T0314587

Perfect Confidence

Jan Ferguson has spent many years working with individuals, groups and organisations to help them achieve their potential. She is an accredited officiant of the British Humanist Association and conducts funeral, wedding, civil partnership and baby naming ceremonies. Jan believes that happiness can be experienced regardless of circumstances not just because of them.

Other titles in the *Perfect* series

Perfect
Confidence

Jan Ferguson

BOOKS

Published by Random House Books 2009

10 9 8 7 6 5 4 3 2 1

Copyright © Jan Ferguson 2009

Jan Ferguson has asserted her right under the Copyright, Designs
and Patents Act 1988 to be identified as the author of this work.

This book is sold subject to the condition that it shall not, by
way of trade or otherwise, be lent, resold, hired out, or otherwise
circulated without the publisher's prior consent in any form of
binding or cover other than that in which it is published and
without a similar condition, including this condition,
being imposed on the subsequent purchaser.

A previous edition of this book was published as *Perfect Assertiveness* in 2003 by
Random House Business Books.

This edition first published in the United Kingdom in 2009 by
Random House Books
Random House, 20 Vauxhall Bridge Road,
London SW1V 2SA

www.rbooks.co.uk

Addresses for companies within The Random House Group Limited
can be found at: www.randomhouse.co.uk/offices.htm

The Random House Group Limited Reg. No. 954009

A CIP catalogue record for this book
is available from the British Library

ISBN 9781847945693

The Random House Group Limited supports The Forest Stewardship
Council® (FSC®), the leading international forest-certification organisation.
Our books carrying the FSC label are printed on FSC®-certified paper.
FSC is the only forest-certification scheme supported by the leading
environmental organisations, including Greenpeace. Our
paper procurement policy can be found at
www.randomhouse.co.uk/environment

Typeset in Minion by Palimpsest Book Production Limited,
Grangemouth, Stirlingshire

Printed and bound in Great Britain by Clays Ltd, St Ives plc

Contents

Introduction

As you read through this book it should become increasingly apparent that you are the main character of the plot. By the final chapter I hope you will understand and like that character more. If it has achieved its aim then the time you have spent reading and thinking about this book will have helped you to:

- understand more about confidence and its importance for leading a happy, healthy life

- understand more about your emotions and about why you behave in certain ways

- recognise the advantages of making a few changes in order to liberate your potential to be yourself

- use realistic tips for behaving and feeling more confident.

In order to get the most from life, whatever our role, we have to work at sorting out relationships with other people. Confidence helps us to do that and this book will give you lots of ideas on how to become more effective in relating to others in your personal life, at work and in specific situations. However, the first relationship that has to be addressed, often the one we neglect, is with ourselves. The exercises and 'pauses for thought' in these chapters will give you the opportunity to spend some time constructively working on your relationship with yourself.

Whatever we do in life, it is useful to have a 'toolkit' to help us deal with what comes along. In my kit, techniques for being more confident are major tools. In fact as I have learned more about confidence it has become such a light device to carry that I am often not aware of it being there.

Two cautionary notes before you go any further into these pages: first, it might seem that I am saying it is easy to be confident. Well, often it isn't easy at all. The important thing is that although it isn't easy it *is* worth it. When you get it right it is a great feeling and it gives you yet more confidence to tackle further issues. But, when it doesn't work, don't be too hard on yourself. Failing is bad enough without punishing yourself for it. Many people who are admired for their confidence confess to sometimes feeling far from confident. I occasionally remind myself of a swan, gliding serenely and calmly, while underneath, where nobody can see, I'm paddling like mad.

The second word of caution is not to take it all too seriously. That of course implies not taking yourself too seriously. Yes, we are looking at personal development, but it is essential to retain a sense of humour and perspective about the whole thing. We've all got hopes, fears, strengths, weaknesses, successes and failures, but we're only people.

Part one

Understanding confidence

1   What is confidence?

Confidence is what you see and what you feel. In the introduction I referred to the swan analogy: there are many people out there who, on the surface, look as though they are coping effortlessly but are in fact paddling hard. So what makes them look confident? It may be a calm self-assurance, it may be an assertive manner, or it may be an air of boldness. You will have your own answer to this question. We are all individual; each of us expresses and perceives confidence in a different way. It is not necessarily true that the most noticeable person in a room or the most talkative in a group is the most confident one.

It is important to establish that we are addressing confidence, not aggressive selfishness. True confidence is a happy, comfortable state of being; it doesn't rely on putting others down or measuring ourselves against other people. It involves respecting yourself and other people. It is possible to be 'overconfident' and that might have all sorts of results. When we are among other people it's important to be sensitive to the effect we are having on them. Sometimes people come over as arrogant and cocky, traits which sometimes mask lack of confidence. A measure of real confidence is how well people relate to others, their level of rapport and their awareness of how others are feeling. Rapport is a tool which will help you to behave more confidently and is discussed in chapter eight.

Another example of overconfidence is that people sometimes have unrealistic expectations of their abilities. I confess to sometimes underestimating how long a task will take and therefore I'm occasionally under pressure to meet a deadline. This makes life harder for myself and it can also cause problems for others. It is therefore an aspect of confidence that I need to examine and modify.

Confidence that only considers our own needs can be selfish and aggressive. Healthy competition and personal ambition are acceptable and necessary in our society, but real confidence balances fairness and consideration with determination to succeed. It is neither passive, giving in to other people's needs, nor aggressive, only considering our own needs, but a comfortable, assertive and respectful centre from which we can be the best we can be.

Different people behave confidently in different ways. It is not a skill for cloning. The glory of human beings is that we are all so different. Our uniqueness is a treasure to be celebrated. We don't have to portray confidence in the same way as somebody else does, but we can be aware of our own self, informed about the concept of confidence and determined to live our life in a way that allows us to achieve goals, fulfil our potential and be happy.

As you go through this book you will be invited to do some thinking about yourself and be offered suggestions on how behaving differently might be more effective for you. It is not, however, a step-by-step guide on how to run your life. Being yourself is the key to happiness and the more you understand about yourself, your behaviour and the behaviour of others, the more opportunity you have to be at your best.

Confidence and control

An important feature in our ability to be confident is having confidence in other people and in situations. Sometimes we need to trust that things around us will be all right. We can only control ourselves and by doing that we can hope to have control of a situation. Often, though, people use energy trying to control another person's behaviour or even their thoughts. We try to control outcomes to situations, whether it be that everybody must enjoy a party or agree with our proposals. Yes, we can influence events in a positive way, but when we try to control them we run out of energy, we become critical and we lose confidence.

What you see

Take a few minutes now to think of somebody who you think looks confident. What is it about them that gives you that impression? Maybe it's to do with posture, the way they dress, their stature or a general presence. Maybe it's about how attractive you think they are. We often hold the misconception that somebody we perceive as beautiful or good-looking oozes confidence. This says more about us than the other person. Beauty is skin-deep, it may have several advantages but confidence is not necessarily one of them.

When people are confident they look as though they are in control of themselves and situations. Imagine the person who comes into a meeting, papers hugged to their chest, head down, muttering a greeting. Do you think, 'Aha! This person is going to have something interesting to say,' or do you dismiss them without a thought? Maybe you've not come across anybody like this, but then again, perhaps you haven't noticed them!

On the other hand, somebody who enters the room full of their own self-importance, hustling people to make a start and obviously determined to put their own needs first is likely to turn people off for different reasons.

When we behave confidently we give the impression of being comfortable with ourselves and happy to occupy the space we stand in. The effect of this impression on other people is that they also feel happy and comfortable around us.

The person who walks into a meeting looking organised, making eye contact with a friendly smile and a greeting, is going to have a far more favourable effect. We are likely to warm to them and actually look forward to hearing what they have to say, not feel threatened by them. Of the three, this is the person who is most likely to achieve their aims confidently.

Exercise

What about you? Which one of these approaches is nearest to describing how you would behave? Write 'yes', 'no' or 'sometimes' in answer to the following:

1. Do you make comfortable eye contact with people when you greet them?

2. If you join a group of people do you scan round to acknowledge all of its members and establish your presence?

3. In general, do you stand or sit with your head up, shoulders relaxed, arms and hands in an open posture?

4. Do you show interest in people by smiling and responding to them?

Sometimes it can be helpful to consider specific situations in more detail. Think about the following questions:

1. What do you look like when you are confident?

2. How does that compare with how you look when you don't feel confident?

3. In which circumstances or situations do you feel confident?

4. When do you lack confidence?

5. What one circumstance would help you to transfer the comfort and confidence from one situation to another?

Perhaps your answer to the last question is that another person would not be present, or would behave differently. Well, sorry, that's not an option! You can only control yourself, not anybody else. Accepting and going with that concept is a big step towards confidence. It means there's less to do, and what a relief that can be!

What you feel

How do you feel when you are confident? Are you happy, relaxed, capable and valued? Maybe you answer 'yes' to some or all of these. On the other hand, maybe you don't really think about it. That's the point really: when we do feel confident in ourselves and in our circumstances we tend not to think about it.

Consider a time when you have done something well. Now think of a time when things didn't go so well. Which of these situations do you remember most clearly? Is it easier to recall the bad feelings left over from the negative experience or the good feelings from the positive one?

Most people would relate to remembering the bad things more strongly. That in itself is one of the reinforcements of lack of confidence. We need to learn from our mistakes, lick our wounds and move on, rather than allowing that critical little voice to creep in saying we've failed. The pattern of negative thinking is as follows: we have a bad experience, we dwell on it, we bring it to mind when we've got something similar to do, it makes us nervous, we have a bad experience . . . and so it goes on. It's important to break this chain and replace negative self-criticism with realistic, encouraging self-praise.

It's a fact of life that there are situations, circumstances and relationships which are difficult; this is true for everybody. Job interview, doctor's appointment, party, journey, meeting: it can be a very long list of challenges that have to be overcome. Some we sail through confidently with little thought, but others cause anxiety, nervousness and even dread. It's horrible when these negative feelings take over and can often lead to a feeling of being out of control.

So what does anxiety feel like? In extreme cases, anxiety can cause panic attacks and illness. Less extreme symptoms are butterflies in the stomach, tense muscles and a dry mouth: you may have your own to add to the list. Alongside these physical feelings we also have to cope with our thoughts. Unfortunately, just at the time when we need a kind internal voice to reassure us that things will be fine, the opposite happens. We start to tell ourselves, very convincingly, that we won't cope, that we will look stupid, basically that we will fail. Why are we so cruel to ourselves? I hope that as you read further you will find ways of minimising the power of this negative self-talk and increasing your confidence.

Features of confidence

I have chosen not to talk specifically about 'confident people' and 'non-confident people' because I think everybody lacks confidence sometimes. Some find it easier than others, some days its easier than other days and sometimes lack of confidence creeps up when we least expect it. It's more helpful to think of some qualities that can be particularly apparent when people are feeling confident:

- They are good to be with.

- They are generally happy within themselves.

- They are in control but not controlling.

- They feel equal to others regardless of differences in skills, status or background.

- They know it is human to make mistakes.

- They encourage confidence in others.

- They treat people well.

- They communicate assertively.

- They know their limitations.

- They accept praise graciously and criticism constructively.

- They prepare for difficult situations.

- They don't tend to analyse everything.

- They don't feel intimidated by people.

Confidence and self-esteem

When confidence is low it affects self-esteem. We can actually feel worthless. This is a horrible relationship to have with anybody, let alone yourself who you have to be with 24/7! You are not worthless, you are a valuable human being with strengths and weaknesses and you will become more confident by caring for yourself and learning some strategies to build your confidence.

Here's your first strategy – a new mantra:

> *I am a valuable human being with strengths and weaknesses and I will become more confident by caring for myself and learning strategies to build my confidence.*

Step 1 – Repeat this to yourself in your head as often as you can.

Step 2 – Practise saying it aloud as often as possible.

Step 3 – Look in a mirror, give yourself a smile and speak the words.

Step 4 – Hold your head up, take a deep breath and say it to somebody you like.

Take as long as you like between the steps. After the first step it might start to feel a bit crazy, but the more you practise the easier it will become. If this isn't your style at all then don't give up on this book – there will be lots more suggestions for coping skills and you will definitely find some that suit your personality.

Low self-esteem prevents us from being who we really are. Sometimes people who are funny, people who are creative and talented, and people who are clever all fail to show these qualities to the world because they don't value the qualities and so don't value themselves. This is sad for them and a loss to those around them, as their contributions could benefit others.

Self-esteem affects our relationship with ourselves and also with others. Think about a situation where you have been in a disagreement with somebody and you have failed to state your point of view. How do you feel afterwards? Angry? Put down? Do you replay the whole incident adding what you could or should have said and frequently chastise yourself for not having done so? You may become more and more angry, but really the anger is not with the other person; it is with yourself – for not standing your ground, for not being quick-witted, articulate or brave enough to counter the attack, however subtle, from the other person. 'Why did I let them speak to me like that?' 'Why didn't I just say . . . ?' 'Who do they think they are?' The more we chew it over the more we eat into our self-esteem. We feel that we have let ourselves down and allowed someone to 'get the better of us'. The incident leaves a sour aftertaste. On the other hand, when we find ourselves in a potentially difficult situation with somebody and we handle it well, we walk away feeling good about ourselves. Which one of these feelings lasts longest? It is usually the negative feelings that hang around.

When we are confident we feel good about ourselves because we let other people know how they can treat us. We don't feel intimidated by other people because we have a realistic, healthy measure of our own self-worth.

Exercise

Chapter five will give you the opportunity to work on your own self-esteem and confidence (see page 47), but as a little taster write down something about you which makes it worth spending time and effort caring for yourself and learning some strategies to build your confidence:

I am worthwhile because . . .

Your 'best self'

Within the core of each of us is a 'best self'. That best self emerges when we are with people we feel comfortable with and in situations where we feel capable and in control. When we are confident we are able to express what we think, what we feel and what we want. In order to do this we have to put some thought into really understanding what it is we think, feel and want. This can mean that you have to let go of some attitudes, habits or behaviours: after all, with every gain there is loss. As you learn more about yourself and confidence, you will be able to weigh up what your profit and loss will be when you are handling situations more confidently. I hope you balance your books to achieve a huge net gain!

Remember, whether you think you can, or whether you think you can't, you're right!

2 Why confidence matters

We need confidence in order to set goals and achieve success, however large or small those goals are and whatever success means to us. This is a competitive world and it is confident people who usually get to win. Whether in sport, the arts, business, running a home and family or having a good social life, confidence is cited as an essential ingredient to success. Confidence enables us to take risks and to participate fully in society, thus helping us to make the most of life. Confidence helps us to express what we want and to assert our needs. It also inspires confidence in others. Confidence is enriching because it means we fulfil our own needs and so have lots to give to other people.

Confidence to be yourself

You are the best you've got. It is important to learn and grow and become increasingly better at living while accepting who you genuinely are and liking that person. This is fundamental to being confident. Lack of confidence often comes from trying to be someone we are not, which is exhausting. Once you accept that the best you have to bring to any situation is yourself then you can, if necessary, do the preparation required in order to make sure it's your best self that you are presenting. If you are going to spend time with friends who like you and who you like, then there should be no preparation required because it is you they want to be with. At the other end of the scale though, if you have to go for a job interview or make a wedding speech then you need to do the work beforehand. In all situations it is you going about your life, and the more relaxed, happy, open and honest you can be with yourself and others, the more confident you will appear.

When we are lacking in confidence, some of the feelings we experience might include:

- embarrassment and awkwardness

- fear

- guilt and blame

- awe of confident people

- insignificance

- isolation and loneliness

- a sense of having been let down or misunderstood

- powerlessness

- pessimism

- physical sickness

- tension.

This is not a finite list and I'm not saying that everybody feels all of these all of the time, but I think we have all had some of these feelings some of the time. When something big and bad happens in life, and of course big, bad things happen to everybody now and then, these feelings become more acute. The experience of loss, whether it's loss of a loved one, a job, a relationship or a physical ability, can seriously affect our confidence. At such times we need to learn to treat ourselves even more gently than usual, but human nature is such that when we need our confident self most it seems to have temporarily deserted us. This is why real, fundamental confidence is what we must work towards. Not superficial bravado but a self-esteem which fills us and that we can call on through good times and bad.

Anxiety

It is very normal to feel anxious. Sometimes anxiety or fear is helpful if it sharpens our awareness of dangerous situations and provokes us into avoiding or dealing with them. Frequently though anxiety is not so useful and is a result of thoughts that don't really have a rational foundation. This is not to say that these thoughts are unimportant; quite the reverse. Job interviews, public speaking, social occasions, asking somebody out, joining an evening class, using public transport . . . The list of activities that cause anxiety is long. Of course not everybody who suffers from being anxious will do so in all of these situations. Many people who perform in the arts have real difficulties with coping with small groups of strangers. Conversely, people who are extremely articulate and influential in small meetings can go to pieces when they have to address a crowd.

There are two aspects to anxiety: what goes on in the body and what goes on in the mind. The physical feelings of anxiety might include a raised heartbeat, sweating, feeling nauseated and going red. Although these feelings are unpleasant and distressing, it's important to accept that they are not dangerous. Also, apart from reddening of the skin, usually nobody else will realise that you are experiencing these symptoms. Learning basic skills of breathing and relaxation will help to control them, and it's helpful to try and recognise that they will pass.

The mental or cognitive aspects of anxiety are those messages that we play in our head, such as, 'I can't talk to strangers. I never know what to say. I always look stupid', 'I'll get into the interview room and my mind will go blank' or 'I can't ask her out – I'll go all red and she'll think I'm stupid and pathetic.'

Nobody's life is completely free of anxiety, depression or self-doubt; these are all part of being human. What is important is to be able to recognise and challenge when you are adding to your problems by what your brain is telling you. Automatic thoughts, usually based on negative criticism of yourself, need to be challenged and changed. If you feel that this is a big problem for you then help is available through Cognitive Behavioural Therapy, a process that teaches people to challenge unhelpful, anxious thoughts and replace them with positive, realistic internal messages which help rather than destroy your confidence. (See the Quick Reference section on page 163 for contact details.)

Here are some examples of confidence-reducing ways of thinking:

- 'All or nothing' thinking – an event is going to be either a *total* success or *total* failure.

- Over-generalising – you once had a bad experience in this kind of situation therefore it will always be like that.

- Exaggerating – reacting to something irritating or embarrassing as though it were a major disaster.

- Catastrophising – imagining that the worst will happen.

- Discounting the positive – refusing to recognise your strengths, the esteem others hold you in and the extent of your capabilities.

Next time you catch yourself indulging in such a thought process, challenge yourself and replace your thoughts with more realistic and enabling self-talk, such as the following examples:

- Human beings sometimes make mistakes, the person who never made a mistake never made anything. I'm a human being.

- I've done a good enough job with this task; it doesn't have to be perfect.

- I've coped before and I can do it again.

- If someone else can do it, then so can I.

- I will accept compliments and praise graciously (otherwise I'm devaluing another person's opinion of me).

- Other people find this hard too. I'm not alone.

- This too will pass!

Crisis of confidence – confidence in crisis

However great the strides you make towards a more confident you, there will always be times in your life when you might experience a blip. Stuff happens; sometimes an event, a revelation, a person's behaviour or a life crisis can throw us off-beam and make us very wobbly. It may have crept up on you slowly or hit you suddenly rather like an electric shock. Just because this has happened, it doesn't mean you have to experience a complete loss of power: the fundamental you is still there, it just can't be accessed so easily for a while.

You may have heard the phrase 'He looks like he's had the stuffing knocked out of him', referring to somebody who has suffered a shock or is going through big problems. This is an apt metaphor because that is exactly what happens to us. If the 'stuffing' is self-esteem, then during these bad times it can feel like yours has been drained away. 'I was gutted' is another phrase we use; that feeling of emptiness, literally as though your guts have been removed and left you with self-doubt, uncertainty and fear. In such extreme cases of lack of confidence it might be wise to seek help. However, whatever you do, hang on to yourself; this is when you need to treat yourself gently. It may be helpful to think about how you would treat a close friend if they were going through this crisis, and follow the advice you would give to them.

Confidence is contagious

Yes, you can catch it. When we are around people who are confident with themselves and with the situation they are in it can help us to gain confidence. If seemingly confident people make you feel inadequate then I suggest you check whether confidence is really what they have, or just a fullness of themselves that doesn't embrace other people's needs and feelings.

Seek out the company of happily confident people. Study their behaviour, try mirroring how they are and you could find yourself feeling just as confident as they look.

3 Where does your confidence come from?

I am often asked whether some people are 'naturally' more confident than others and whether I believe that confidence is instinctive in some people. This is the 'big one' – the debate about nature versus nurture in personality and behaviour. Have we inherited our characteristics or are we the product of our environment? Is it the ingredients or the temperature of the oven that results in the best outcome?

My personal view is that we are a mixture of both of these fundamental influences. We've all inherited characteristics and traits which form part of our genetic make-up; we've all had experiences which have influenced our personality and behaviour. Some of us have been luckier than others, but above all, we are all equipped with the capacity for change. We are not fixed into certain patterns of thought or behaviour. If we believe too rigidly that the influence of either nature or nurture has set our behavioural destiny, then that belief can become an explanation and an excuse for why we can't change and do things differently.

Some people retreat from taking positive steps that would improve their life. They build a protective comfort zone around themselves from which they inhabit life. Stepping out of that comfort zone is very difficult, even though life within the zone is not necessarily truly comfortable. When people are in counselling or a process of self-development, they sometimes come up against a realisation that highlights a need for changing their behaviour or attitude. Although they can see that the change would bring real benefits to them, it becomes clear that this change is too difficult for them to undertake. This can often be observed in a physical withdrawal: they might fold their arms tightly across their chest, saying, 'Well, this is me; this is the way I am.' Or there is a long 'Mmm . . .' and a nod of the head, usually signifying that they have arrived at this water's edge before but it is always too difficult to take the plunge so they are going to retreat once again.

Perhaps you can relate to this by looking back on a number of New Year's resolutions you have made and broken over the years. Knowing what needs to change is not the same as making it happen.

Is confidence instinctive in some of us? Is it natural behaviour? What is your view? I am certain that it comes more naturally to some than others. I think that once we are aware of what enhances our confidence and helps us to behave more confidently we can call on this awareness and consciously use it. Gradually it becomes internalised as part of our habitual behaviour.

Young children can be instinctively confident. Ask a child of two or three years of age if they want to go for a walk and they will answer yes or no spontaneously. Ask an adult and they will probably say 'Well, what would you like to do?' Through the process of conditioning, children learn that passive behaviour is seen as more acceptable to those around them so in order to gain approval they adapt, losing their natural capacity for asserting their needs confidently. Young children also have a natural capacity for aggression, but once they begin to learn that this is seen as unacceptable to people around them, they will sometimes disguise or subdue this natural aggressiveness, replacing this with other styles of non-assertive behaviour, which can be very manipulative. As people grow up this aggression can be confused with confidence, maybe through sarcasm or disparaging quips which humiliate by making somebody the butt of a so-called joke. Alternatively it can manifest itself in arrogant, dominating characteristics. I have met bullies who consider themselves to be extremely confident until they are helped to examine some of their behaviour and the source of it.

A theory that I find very useful in helping people to gain a better understanding of themselves is that of Transactional Analysis or TA, which was first developed by Eric Berne, an American psychiatrist and psychotherapist. He observed certain patterns of thought and behaviour in his patients and developed his observations into a psychological model which can be very easily explained. Put simply, the theory suggests that each of us has three ego states from which we operate, regardless of our age or status; these are **parent–adult–child** and are always represented like this:

Our **parent** is a mixture of the rules and norms which were passed to us in the early stages of development – the taught element.

Our **child** represents how we received the messages which were going on around us and the feelings which they evoked – the felt element.

Our **adult** is the result of the influences upon us merged with our experiences of life and the perceptions we have reasoned for ourselves – the thought element.

Let's look at each of the ego states before coming back to link the theory with confidence.

Your parent ego state

Imagine that from the day you were born until the age of about ten, a tape recorder was switched on inside your head to record everything it hears from the outside world. Now, find yourself a quiet moment in your surroundings and in your head. Allow yourself to travel on a journey backwards. If you press the play button now on that old tape recording, whose voices will you hear most? Maybe it is one or both of your actual parents, a teacher, a relative, a family friend, an older brother or sister?

Exercise

What sort of messages will be on your recording from birth to about ten? Try to recall and note down some of the actual phrases you hear:

	PERSON	SAYING
example	mother	Don't show yourself up.
example	teacher	We've got high expectations of you; your brother did very well at this school.
1		
2		
3		
4		
5		

It is likely that you have heard a variety of messages, so it's helpful to go back to what you've written and differentiate between positive and negative messages. Some of the messages may be neutral. Put a circle round those you perceive to be negative. Which do you hear most on the tape? Positive, negative or neutral?

Below you'll read some of the typical responses to this exercise. How do they compare with what you have written?

> *'Don't do that', 'do as you're told', 'you're a clever boy', 'because I said so', 'who do you think you are?', 'well done', 'you should know better', 'never trust a . . .', 'wait until your father gets home', 'put your face straight', 'don't let the family down', 'don't show yourself up', 'don't, you'll hurt yourself', 'you must share', 'big boys don't cry', 'learn to stick up for yourself', 'don't raise your voice to me', 'I love you', 'always be polite to your elders', 'never go out looking untidy', 'you're so clumsy', 'don't ask stupid questions'.*

Many of the messages on our tape will be 'do' and 'don't' messages, laying down rules, probably with little or no explanation. Some will be cautionary ('mind you don't fall', 'watch the road') and some will be instructive ('be polite', 'be nice and share'). Many of those you remember clearly are likely to be critical of you and may have been internalised as part of your belief system about life and about yourself. These recorded messages form a strong part of our personality and influence our behaviour as adults in two major ways: replaying the messages to ourselves and communicating the messages to others.

Consider the impact of some of these messages when we are trying to cope with life as grown-ups. It is often said that public speaking is at the top of many people's biggest fear list. If messages such as 'you shouldn't boast', 'don't show off', 'who do you think you are?' are strongly recorded on your tape then it is likely that your own parent ego state will subconsciously replay that message, the result being that just the thought of being the centre of attention can send you into panic and dread. The voices on these recordings are people to whom we looked for wisdom and authority when we were forming our own self-image. If they told us frequently that we weren't clever enough, that we should control ourselves rather than show emotions, that we mustn't question authority or that we were a nuisance, then those messages are likely to have influenced how we feel about ourselves as adults. This often makes us harder on ourselves than we are on other people, finding it difficult to be forgiving or accepting of our own shortcomings.

One way we replay our negative parental messages is through the 'I should/I must' game, which goes something like this:

> *'I must ask so-and-so round', 'I should be nicer to my mother-in-law', 'I should be better at this', 'I mustn't draw attention to myself', 'I must put others first', 'I must look as though I can cope', 'I should clean out the garage', 'I must stay looking like I can cope', 'I should go and visit so-and-so', 'I must finish this before I sit down', 'I must show them that I'm as good as they are', 'I must look immaculate', 'I mustn't upset anybody'.*

Exercise

Try to add some of your own 'musts' and 'shoulds' to these examples.

'Musts' and 'shoulds' serve to reinforce the set of values imposed on us through actual parental messages, even though we are now adults who are aware that not all of these rules and values are still relevant to our own life today. Many of these values are essential as a code of morality or as personal principles, others will help us to achieve and be successful in life. However, the negative aspects – which cause us to be too hard on ourselves – also continue to play. This gets in the way of really developing ourselves; it stops us from confidently and rationally believing that we have the right to assert ourselves, to express what we think and feel, or to behave in the way that is truly being ourselves.

An example of interfering parental messages can be seen with Sue and David, a 'thirty-something' professional couple whose small baby was taken into hospital. The hospital staff were casual and uncommunicative. After several days there was a worrying lack of urgency and efficiency in the treatment. Sue and David, both confident, articulate people, were deeply anxious about their baby yet were reluctant to appear 'pushy' or critical in expressing concern to the hospital staff. They both held the belief that doctors know best and that we must be grateful for anything nurses do because they are so overworked. This belief held them back from questioning and expressing their alarm. Parental messages regarding authority, polite behaviour and gratitude got in the way of the need to assertively question authority. You see, even though they were actual parents, responsible for their baby, their own parental messages were still playing in the background and influencing their behaviour. (You'll be pleased to hear that baby is fine and Sue and David have helped each other to do a bit of work on their ego states and confidence!)

Changing negative messages

When our 'internal tape recording' is playing to reinforce the criticism we have heard as children it lowers our self-esteem and confidence. Those negative messages which you identified earlier in the chapter serve to 'put you in your place' even though the place you are entitled to occupy now, as an adult, is very different from your status as a child. It is hardly surprising that you will find it difficult to express what you really think, feel and want from others if the parental message you keep hearing is telling you that you are unimportant, unworthy, a nuisance or not entitled to question others.

Exercise

Go back to each of the critical messages which you identified in the table earlier and ask yourself the following, making a note of your answers:

1. Is this true about me now?

2. Do I sometimes replay this message and allow it to influence the way I behave?

3. Why does this prevent me from being confident?

4. I don't need to play this message any more because . . .

Sending negative messages to others

When we communicate to other people we sometimes do so directly from our parent ego state; this is particularly likely when we are criticising somebody. Rather than offering constructive feedback, we tend to come across as aggressive. There are a lot of absolute statements associated with this ego state, such as 'You have no right . . .', 'You should be . . .', 'You're always . . .', 'You never . . .' These absolute statements are judgements, as if our view is the one right way of looking at things and therefore needs to be heeded.

Can you think of a time when you have heard yourself saying something to a child and realised that the words and the tone of voice are exactly the same as those you were once used to hearing? I remember when one of my daughters first appeared wearing 'real' make-up. I found myself saying, 'What have you got all that muck on your face for? You're pretty enough without it.' On reflection I found my response shocking. The words and tone of voice exactly mimicked my grandmother. My rational, adult self knows that make-up can be fun; experimenting is part of being young, but my reaction was a put-down. The result of this kind of message, particularly if it is frequently heard by a young person, could be to stifle their creativity and their confidence to explore different styles. Or it could cause strong rebellion which might result in aggressive rather than confident behaviour. Either way, it's unhelpful and not the right way to nurture and help a young person to become a happy, confident adult.

In work situations, when senior people give out this sort of parental message to their staff, it causes feelings of humiliation and rebelliousness. Remember, the parent ego state is not to do with age or being an actual parent. It is one of the aspects of our personality which influences the way we are. Children and young people also can behave in the parent state; if you listen to small children playing, you will hear them communicating from their parent state, repeating messages which have been recorded on their tape.

Exercise

Write down some of the things you do or say now as an adult which you have copied from one of your parents or somebody who was influential in your childhood. For example, is there any real scientific evidence to support the old adage. 'Don't put your coat on until you get outside or you won't feel the benefit'?

It is from the parent ego state that we can appear to be domineering or patronising and to put people down. As we have seen, the parent ego state is not always in line with the reality of the present. Furthermore, it neglects the fact that other people perceive life differently from us. Our parent state tends to communicate from an assumption that only our perception is correct. The high expectations – the 'shoulds' and 'musts' of our own parent ego states – might not be relevant or compatible with other people's experience of parent messages.

An example of this can seen with Gerald, who had worked in engineering since leaving school. Now, at 43, he had been made redundant and found unemployment a devastating experience. He was willing to do any kind of work just to 'be useful' again, and started signing-on at the job centre.

Gerald was horrified when he listened to some of the people there, hearing that they had never had a job and weren't really interested in any of the 'situations vacant' on display. Consequently his attitude to the people was unpleasant and abusive. He had no perception of the fact that not working was the norm for these people, as it had been for other people in their families when they were young. Their parental messages were quite different from Gerald's but he showed prejudice towards them and became more angry about his own situation, rather than accepting them at face value and confidently going about his own business.

Remember, we do not see things as they are, we see things as we are.

How the parent prevents self-confidence

Old habits die hard. Our parent ego state expresses thoughts that have become internalised. This is never more true than when we are actually parenting our own children. If we continue to give them rules, with little or no logical explanation, at some stage in their development these rules cause argument. Because they genuinely don't understand any reason for the rules they will start to confront and question our authority. Backed to the wall, our parent ego state becomes even stronger and so a state of conflict emerges.

In work situations, managers whose control of their staff is parent-based risk the result of people merely doing as they are told, rather than taking initiative and working creatively.

Communicating in the parent ego state

What people say and the way they say it can give us clues to the ego state from which they are speaking. When we are in our parent state we will have a tendency to sound like some of the following:

- Authoritarian – 'This is the way things are.'

- Stubborn – 'I'm not interested in your opinion.'

- Pompous – 'In my day you wouldn't have got away with this.'

- Condescending – 'I knew I should have done it myself.'

- Threatening – 'You'd better put it right or else.'

- Controlling – 'You will do as I say.'

When we come to look at the adult ego state we will see that there is an assertive alternative to this hierarchical attitude.

Your child ego state

Having explored your parent ego state you are now invited to think about the child aspect of this theory. We said that the child ego state is that which is determined by how we felt the world around us to be when we were very young, rather than what we thought about it. Imagine now that there was a second tape, this time recording what you were feeling during your early years, not what you heard. Think about what it is like being a young person; what are the feelings experienced by toddlers and children? Some examples are **happy**, sad, scared, **excited**, jealous, 'that's not fair', compliant, curious, frustrated, **confused**, **sulky**, **angry**, **affectionate**, **loving**, inferior, rebellious. (I will explain why some are bold later.)

Exercise

Now add some of your own feelings to the list above.

These feelings are still part of us; the blueprint exists within ourselves to re-experience them. When faced with difficulties, criticisms, threats or a fun environment our behaviour is triggered by one of these feelings.

The free child and the adapted child

There are two aspects of the child state, and each of us has a certain amount of both. Go back to the words you used to describe feelings. The words in the previous list in bold type represent behaviour that comes from the free child. This is the part of us which is likely to be creative, to enjoy partying, to rebel against authority and to lose our temper. Allowing the free child to emerge occasionally offers a healthy response to the stresses and strains of life. When we take everything, including ourselves, too seriously we lose sight of some of the spontaneity of life.

People express their free child in different ways, such as singing, dancing, hugging, laughing, crying, being creative and partying. These all link in to a natural confidence and sense of well-being.

Exercise

1. How do you express your free child?

2. Which of these activities do you do regularly?

3. Which of them did you used to do but have got out of the habit of doing?

4. In what ways would the quality of your overall well-being improve if you found more time to enjoy some of these pleasures?

5. So, what are you going to do about this?

Being emotionally and physically expressive is part of being confident. It demonstrates a positive attitude in which life, regardless of its difficulties and sadness, is seen as an opportunity, not a threat. After all, life is all we've actually got. If we live with one foot in the past (regretting) and one foot in the future (feeling anxious) then we miss the present. Much of the 'free child' activity described above involves the here and now – being alive for the moment.

The examples above represent the positive aspects of the free child, but it is unrealistic not to mention that there are also some negative aspects which can get in the way of being confident. When we were children, we may have given vent to anger, jealousy and frustration by striking out at another person or behaving manipulatively in some way. This spontaneous behaviour is likely to be anti-social because it is totally selfish, having no regard for the rights and feelings of the other person. Whether it manifests itself in aggression or manipulation it will usually lead to difficult relationships. If the other person is also behaving from their free child state, there is the possibility that you may have a good fight, get it out of your system and clear the air. But in more formal relationships this is rarely the way things happen.

If you are interested in learning more about ego states and communication I recommend that you read some of the excellent books available on Transactional Analysis from the further reading section at the back of this book (see page 163).

The other aspect of the child ego state is influenced by the way we have learned to help ourselves feel more comfortable through adapting to other people's needs and expectations of us. If, as a small child, you were given rewards or 'positive strokes' for behaving in a gentle, quiet, unobtrusive way, then that is likely to be your general demeanour as an adult. Anger is an emotion which in our culture is seen as negative and 'naughty'. If you have been punished for showing and expressing anger then it is likely that you will have adapted that behaviour in order to avoid punishment. This can often lead to a sulky, sullen response to situations we don't like or don't agree with. As we will see in chapter six, some people are very nervous of conflict. If, when you play the 'feelings' tape recording from your childhood, there is fear and anxiety on that tape, then you are likely to avoid situations that might recall that state because you don't have the confidence to deal with them: even though you are a real grown-up, you still hold on to the vulnerability of being a child.

It is the adapted child ego state which evokes the desire to please others. While this is a wonderful and generous trait, you know enough about confidence by now to hear alarm bells. Pleasing others is only possible if we are also able to please ourselves. Being able to say 'no' and express our own needs is vital. This ego state contributes enormously to lack of confidence – what we must learn is that we are not the vulnerable child being threatened by big important people any more. We are thinking, capable grown-ups with rights, who are willing to accept other people's rights and work towards comfortable, compatible relationships.

William is an example of someone with a prevalent adapted child ego state. He's an efficient and highly numerate middle-aged insurance administrator but has constantly been overlooked for promotion. His employers describe him as honest, hard-working, dependable, and 'a whizz with figures'. Yet, after 16 years in the same job he has seen junior people overtake him to achieve promotions into jobs that he is technically capable of doing. During an appraisal with a new boss, it became clear that William lacked the confidence and self-assurance needed to complement the technical aspects required for promotion to a more senior job in the company. It transpired that William had missed a lot of schooling as a child due to his parents' lack of interest in education. When he did attend school he was faced with a partic-ularly harsh form teacher who humiliated and taunted William by continually goading him to account for his absence. William had learned very astutely to stay out of authority's way, keep his head down and do the best he could. This is what he brought to his working life and this was how he was perceived by employers and colleagues. Of course they all described him as 'hard-working and dependable' – he never said 'no' to anything and often took work home. William's adapted child ego state was prevalent and as an adult he continued to see people in authority as powerful.

In their presence his feelings replayed the tape of fear and humiliation.

Exercise

1. Can you recall a time when you, as a child, were subjected to humiliation, either from a parent, teacher, older child or another adult? Can you remember and describe your feelings at the time?

2. Are there situations like this that you now experience as an adult but still cause you to feel like this?

3. Are there any people, or types of people, who you still feel like this with?

4. What are you going to do to make sure that these very real and understandable feelings don't get in the way when you would like to feel and present yourself as a confident person?

William's manager sent him on an assertiveness training course, where he learned to look at his strengths and to role-play situations in which he stood up to people who were supposedly more clever and powerful than himself.

Remember, nobody can make you feel inferior without your permission.

Communicating in the child ego state

When we are in our child ego state we will have a tendency to sound like some of the following:

- Complaining, moaning, whining – 'That's not fair.'

- Challenging – 'Mine's better than yours.'

- Demanding – 'I want . . .'

- Bargaining – 'I will if you will.'

- Sulking – 'It's not my fault/that's not fair.'

- Angry – Slamming doors, stamping feet.

- Complying – 'All right then.'

When, in the adult world, we are faced with situations where, subconsciously, we re-experience our childlike feelings, we behave in our child state. This explains why we occasionally react in a manner that is totally disproportionate to what is actually happening. Something triggers feelings of threat, humiliation, anger or sense of unfairness and we behave rather like a grown-up equivalent of lying down on the supermarket floor screaming, or we take our ball away so that nobody else can play!

Your adult ego state

The adult ego state is probably what you operate in most of the time. It is the part of us which has thought about and learned from experiences – that has formed our own framework and attitudes to how we live our lives and how we accept other people. Our adult state is not judgemental of others; it accepts our own fallibility and takes account of our own and other people's rights. The adult element responds to what is actually going on; it is a rational response to behaviour based on taking in the messages that are being transmitted here and now. This ego state relies on knowledge and experience; it helps us to behave objectively. It is the adult ego state which enables us to behave confidently, not requiring that we defend ourselves or attack somebody else.

Communicating in the adult ego state

When we are in our adult ego state, we will probably use some of the following:

- Reasoning – 'I see your point of view.'

- Problem-solving – 'What do you think is the way forward here?'

- Disclosing – 'I am upset and disappointed about this.'

- Making criticism – 'My view is that it wasn't handled well.'

- Clarifying – 'Can I check if we both see this the same way?'

Now think about how much more confident these examples come across than those listed for the parent and the child ego states.

Exercise

Try to identify from which ego state each of the following statements about Transactional Analysis have been made:

1. 'This is a load of rubbish, I've got by all my life without learning about this TA business.'

2. 'This sounds interesting. I wonder if it can offer a new approach to solving a personality clash which is going on at work at the moment.'

3. 'I'd better learn about this in case the person who lent me this book expects me to have an intelligent discussion about it.'

4. 'I'm going to read a bit more about this, I think it could be helpful to me.'

5. 'Whoopee! Does this mean it's all right for me to get drunk at the office party this year?!'

A healthy individual needs a mixture of all three ego states to take them successfully through life's journey. Your parent state is the basic map on which the routes, dangers and opportunities are written. Sometimes, the map will be out of date, making it necessary to question it by exploring routes from the thinking, reasoning and objectivity which is your adult. Your child state is your experience of the journey: the willingness to delight in the opportunities, explore new territories, risk new approaches and feel the emotions of living.

Understanding more about ourselves gives us more choices about how we can behave: strengthening our adult aspect increases our ability to feel and behave with confidence. The aim of TA is to increase our adult state but, in doing so, not to obliterate the child or parent states; it is sufficient to be aware of them and be able to acknowledge that behaviour rooted in one of those ego states might not always be appropriate for the situation at the time.

ANSWERS: 1. Parent; 2. Adult; 3. Adapted child; 4. Adult; 5. Free child

4 The right to be confident

Human nature tends to make us modest. People are not generally comfortable with saying what they are good at. Whatever you do in your life, you have skills and capabilities. You might have real talent as well. Every now and then it's helpful to sit down and catch up on exactly what your skills and capabilities are. Your skills will come from things you might do at work, at home, as a pastime or hobby. Whether they are practical, caring, supportive, intellectual or academic, they all count.

Exercise

Take some time now to think about yourself, your capabilities and your skills. Make a list of them in no particular order. Once you have done this for yourself, ask somebody else what they think your capabilities are.

If you are thinking that learning to become more confident is not easy then I agree with you, even though this book may read as though I am saying it's a piece of cake. Lack of confidence can cause us to behave badly. Ducking out of tricky situations by being passive or striking out aggressively when your back is to the wall is behaviour that comes all too easily. Ask my kids, ask my husband, ask my colleagues, ask my friends and ask the plumbers who caused my kitchen ceiling to fall in!

What I am certain of, though, is that however difficult it is to behave confidently, it is worth the effort. It can lead to a happier, calmer, more fulfilling and joyous existence for the individual and for the people around them. Nobody really likes a wimp, least of all the person who is one! Nobody wants to get close to an aggressive ranter – you wouldn't put your hand into a tiger's cage, would you?

Knowing your rights and responsibilities

Do you have the right to be a confident person? Of course you do. I also believe we have the responsibility to make the most of life by striving to achieve our potential, by being happy and helping those around us to be happy. Knowing your rights as a human being can enable you to behave in a way which leads to greater fulfilment and personal satisfaction. However, it is not only our rights, but also the rights of others that need to be considered.

I was recently working with an organisation in a consultancy role, with the objective of improving their customer service. Once I started to understand the company, it became clear – not unusually – that there was a great deal of internal conflict going on between departments and individuals. My view is that the service received by customers is usually a reflection of what goes on internally; clearly, in this case there was a need for increased co-operation and relationship building. The staff were in agreement with this, so when my colleague and I presented to the board what we intended to do, we put forward the notion of an internal Bill of Rights. Whoops! How much we learn from our mistakes! The Managing Director declared the whole idea as unpalatable; he viewed it as subversive and launched into a tirade of 'the trouble with this country . . . rights . . . too many rights . . .' (Yes, well done if you have identified this as parent ego state.) The upshot was that he didn't really listen to the rest of our presentation and we had to work hard to rebuild credibility.

Maybe you had a similar response when I introduced the word 'rights'. If so, please don't throw the book across the room! When I talk about rights and confidence I mean that these are universal rights and therefore we have the responsibility to respect the rights of other people. To give you an example I would like to present to you what I acknowledge as a 'bill of rights' for co-operative, harmonious living.

Feeling and knowing that I have 'Rights' helps my self-respect and enhances my confidence to 'go for it'. Acknowledging that other people share those rights prevents me from being totally self-centred and ensures that I treat other people with respect.

You may disagree with some of these rights, or wish to add your own. I present them to you as a concept rather than a set of rules. Your values and beliefs will influence the content of your own Bill of Rights. An interesting and worthwhile application of drawing up a Bill of Rights is to do it as a family, as colleagues or as a group of people coming together for whatever reason. The process of this exercise helps us to learn more about one another, appreciate what is important to people and therefore enjoy open, comfortable relationships in which each individual can express their own uniqueness.

Everybody has the right to . . .

1. Ask for what they want.

2. Express their opinions and feelings and show emotion.
Doing this in a confident way will mean doing it in a way appropriate to the situation.

3. Not be discriminated against.
And therefore not to feel inferior for any reason.

4. Make their own decisions and cope with the consequences.
Resist being influenced by what others say we 'should' do.

5. Choose whether or not to get involved with someone else's problems.
Sometimes it is necessary to distinguish between having a responsibility towards others and being responsible for others.

6. Make mistakes.
Learn from them and improve.

7. Get what they pay for.
Whether buying something, employing somebody or using a service.

8. Change their mind.
When we have the confidence to listen well we may realise that somebody else's point of view is right.

9. Privacy of thought, space and personal issues.

10. Be successful.
In our society there is a tendency to play down our achievements. It is OK to be successful and to celebrate success.

A Family Bill of Rights

Family life can bring all sorts of tensions. Some people may feel they are being taken for granted, others may feel that there are too many restrictions. Complicated dynamics are going on and often we don't address them. While parents have responsibility to their children they also have the right to some privacy and personal space. Children need discipline and structure, but they also have the right to explanations of why certain behaviour is or is not acceptable. The process of talking about one another's rights and drawing up a bill or charter can be very illuminating in terms of understanding how each member of the family perceives their own world and their place within that family.

A team charter

A group of people who work together can remove some of the barriers and blocks to effective communication by participating in a discussion based around the notion of 'what is and what isn't OK in this team'. I recently facilitated this with a group of busy people working in an open-plan office; they designed their 'bill'. All sorts of things came out about social chit-chat and disruptive behaviour which clearly had needed saying for some time. The outcome was that people felt more able to ask for quiet, or to move away from time-wasters, without it causing conflict or offence.

Process and content

As with many problem-solving exercises, the process of discussing issues is as valuable as the content of the final Bill of Rights. It will not work well if people are defensive. They need to be open to receive and offer criticism in a constructive, assertive way. (Some techniques for doing this are addressed later in the book.)

People have, on many occasions, found this notion of rights liberating. It has helped them to move forward positively by having greater confidence as a team or family and greater confidence as individuals. This really does lead to a happier state in which people are more fulfilled and waste less energy on the negative stuff of keeping everybody happy on the surface without really fully meeting anybody's needs.

Your right to confidence

Self-esteem is both a cause and an effect of confidence. We could have such a good time learning to work on our weaknesses and celebrate our strengths if only we would let ourselves.

Exercise

Write five positive statement's about your strengths. This time I want you to focus on qualities rather than skills and make sure that what you write is positive.

Think about your qualities, such as I am happy/I am generous/I am loving/I am honest with myself/I am good fun, rather than your skills (I am a good driver/cook/parent/golfer etc.). Don't stop here, if you can think of more please go on writing them down.

Sometimes on assertiveness training or confidence-building courses this task is met with excruciating embarrassment from both men and women. There is a lot of wriggling, pen-chewing, crossing out and head shaking. Of course, there are occasionally a few people who do it immediately and with obvious pleasure. It makes me happy when somebody asks if they have to stop at five!

If you are struggling with this, what would your best friend or somebody close to you write about you? What are the qualities that attract them to you? Not what you do for them, but the essential you, the person you are when you are relaxed, happy and at your best?

When you have completed this task, read through your list of 'I ams', take in a deep breath and appreciate yourself and your right to be confident.

Remember, learn to carve your strengths in marble and write your weaknesses in sand.

Part two

Your confidence toolkit

5 Being more assertive

A lot has been written about whether confidence and assertiveness are the same thing. The way I see it, confidence is the state and assertiveness is the behaviour. When we are feeling confident we are quite naturally assertive, expressing ourselves clearly and respecting other people's views. Lack of confidence is far more likely to result in either passive or aggressive behaviour as we are unsure of ourselves and our abilities. I visualise an arc with passiveness at one end, aggression at the other and assertiveness in the middle. When we feel confident we can move through this arc to use behaviour which is appropriate to the situation. When we lack confidence we sometimes swing from passive to aggressive with unhappy consequences. Have you ever spent a day biting your tongue, feeling put upon or put down and then found yourself taking it out on the kids, the cupboards, the cat or your gear stick?

Although we have evolved from being animals in the jungle we are still equipped with the wonderful capacity to respond to danger with either a 'fight' or 'flight' response. 'Fight' represents aggressive behaviour, while 'flight' is usually passive. It's a different jungle that we operate in now. The 'danger' might be the stress of competing for a parking place, somebody criticising you, the need to speak out in a meeting, dealing with a difficult person or trying to get the customer service desk in Mumbai to help you fix something on your computer. Once we start to feel the stress, or 'danger', of these situations we tend to respond instinctively either by being aggressive and making the problem worse, or passive and backing off to try and make it go away. Either way will usually result in us having regrets later.

When we are confident in a stressful situation, we stay in control and so are able to choose our behaviour. Sometimes it's appropriate to be passive and back down, sometimes we need some aggression but there is a huge difference between our selecting this behaviour and the behaviour selecting us.

A balanced life will always have ups and downs. Feeling those ups and downs, knowing when they are happening to you and choosing the best way to deal with them, promotes a well-being from which we are able to be confident and assertive.

ACT on stress

Awareness: learn about what stress actually is, how it affects you as an individual and how it might be affecting people around you.

Confrontation: of things or people that cause you stress. Doing something about it in order to become more in control. This might involve being more assertive with certain people or in certain situations, it might be about becoming a better time manager or being more organised.

Therapy: treating yourself well. It doesn't have to mean lying on a couch paying somebody to listen to you, although if that is helpful, then why not? It is about recognising that you have needs – remembering the person you are when you are confident and not under stress, living in the present and experiencing the moment, rather than always having one foot on the way to where you've got to go next.

'Stamp collecting'

It is important to try to deal with negative situations rather than store them up and allow them to eat into our confidence. I'd like to introduce you to the notion of 'stamp collecting', a phrase which offers a graphic explanation of how people save up all their angst and then POW! They let somebody have it. Have you been on the receiving end of this? Let's see if it rings any bells.

You may be too young to remember Green Shield stamps. They came in sheets and you had to lick the back of them and stick them into a special book. They were given away with petrol and various products in the same way as we now are offered 'loyalty cards' in order to encourage us to spend more. Once you'd collected several thousand of them, they could be cashed in for a thermos flask or something similar which was probably not relevant to your needs at the time!

Well, think about yourself as you go through the day, the week, the years. Perhaps somebody says or does something to you that you don't like. Rather than responding assertively, you store it up, in other words, you lick a stamp and stick it in your memory book. The same person or somebody else says or does something, and this is another stamp, and so it goes on. After a while you've got a really big collection and every now and then it can be taken out and inspected to assess the hurt, humiliation and frustration other people have caused you – the unfairness of life. Then one day, something snaps and causes you to cash in all of your stamps. You really let somebody have it. It probably isn't one of the people who gave you loads to collect – the amount you cash in with that person is probably disproportionate to their actual contribution to your collection – but nevertheless, they are getting it anyway!

Sound familiar? Can you recall a situation when you have been on the receiving end of this? Can you remember the person's body language and tone of voice? It is likely that at the time they were trying to hurt, humiliate and blame you for their own feelings, while justifying their own righteousness. This kind of behaviour can be seen in all kinds of scenarios.

Let's look at Susan, a mother at home, who feels that she is constantly giving to everybody around her and, consequently, has a lot of unexpressed feelings about her situation, such as resentment, disappointment and frustration. She submerges the feelings – stamp collects them – and then cashes them in over something fairly trivial like a broken glass, muddy feet or a borrowed pair of tights. The receiver of the stamps will be mystified at the outburst over something seemingly trivial and will probably dismiss it as 'nagging'.

Or what about Keith, a supervisor in a shop where the staff enjoy a relaxed, sociable working environment but are rather sloppy in terms of customer attitudes and tidiness. He is aware that staff take advantage of his passive style and one day he criticises a till mistake by issuing stern, non-specific, indiscriminate disciplinary warnings out of the blue. The people receiving these 'stamps' will not know what is actually expected of them. It is unlikely they will retain any respect for Keith or be prepared to change their work habits in response.

Susan and Keith have both allowed themselves to be passive, taking 'flight' by avoiding issues, and so eventually resorted to the other extreme – 'fight'. They've expended the energy which they've been holding in check only because they didn't have the confidence to deal with the issues assertively. If Susan were to point out to her family just what it is she feels she gives to them and tells them what she would like in return, then a dialogue could begin to take them forward and bypass barriers of resentment.

Keith needs to tell his staff the standards that are expected of them and ensure that he gives constructive feedback, rather than stamp collecting when standards are not maintained.

By storing up hurt and humiliation we can build a 'case' for ourselves and justify negative feelings about other people. We may have been taught that anger is unacceptable and learned to shy away from conflict. The act of cashing in our collection of stamps will probably mean displacing the anger – towards the wrong person, in the wrong situation, with a disproportionate response to one particular incident. There might be a short-term reward to this in terms of 'getting it off your chest' but the longer-term consequences are likely to be uncomfortable, either in your feelings about yourself or your relationship with the other person. That other person becomes a scapegoat.

Exercise

Are you sitting comfortably? Then maybe this is an opportunity for you to take out your stamp collection. Write down situations or relationships where you can recognise that you have stamp collected.

What can you do now in order to deal assertively with some of the hurt or resentment you might have put down on paper? Having identified these, perhaps by the time you get to the end of this book, you will feel ready to start tackling them. On the other hand, maybe some of them are out of date and irrelevant to your life as it is right now. It might be better for you to let some of these go. Yes, you may have been aggrieved, but nobody ever said life would be fair. Stamp collecting involves time and emotional energy. You have to find somewhere to store the stamps and whenever you come across them you have to indulge in a bit of self-pity. Have you really got so much spare time in your life that you can afford to do this? Never forget that in life there is no dress rehearsal.

Don't collect stamps. Like Green Shield stamps they are things of the past. Learn to choose appropriate behaviour at the time so that you are not swinging like a pendulum from passive to aggressive. Other people are not responsible for our behaviour or our feelings – we are. Assertiveness is about taking responsibility for yourself, not blaming other people for your own unhappiness. If somebody hurts you then you have every right to feel the pain of that hurt, but hanging on to it and allowing it to contaminate your general sense of well-being and confidence is a waste of your life. Others can only affect us as much as we allow them to. Who is in charge of your life? Are your arms raised and your hands free in order to be the conductor of your life, or are they being manipulated like a marionette having its strings pulled?

Remember, you are in charge. You control your feelings. You can make choices about how you respond and behave.

When aggression is the necessary choice

There may be times when choosing to be aggressive will be the most effective or appropriate behaviour. If somebody is being very unpleasant and you want to get rid of them, it may be better to use a degree of aggression. Some situations of sexual harassment or abuse might be avoided if people gave clearer messages about what is unacceptable to them, rather than worrying about offending the other person or being made to look stupid. The main purpose is to get your point across and if somebody is behaving in an aggressively unacceptable way with you it might be appropriate to behave aggressively back. You are in charge. You can choose. We don't have to behave in a certain way because 'that's the way we are'. We can decide which is the best way to behave in order to achieve our object-ive in each specific situation.

Assertiveness in action

Try using some practice situations like negotiating at a car boot sale or asking somebody to give you back a book you have lent them. Doing these successfully will help to build your confi-dence. The effect has a self-fulfilling pattern: you become more assertive in these situations; your self-esteem increases; you become more confident; you behave more assertively . . . and so it goes on. Furthermore, by thinking through situations, you actually become clearer about what you really do and don't want. You are more able to set goals based on how you would really like things to be rather than some vague notion that you don't like the way things are.

We are complicated beings with a tendency to weave compli-cated relationships with people. Sometimes these relationships become so complex that trying to deal with them is rather like trying to untie a very tight, wet knot. Spending time giving constructive thought to this relationship can ensure that your motive and your approach to dealing with it are clear and specific.

Exercise

Write down a situation which you want to deal with assertively. Now write down how you actually feel about this. Next write down how you would like things to be. (Sometimes a useful question to ask yourself here is 'What would life be like if I didn't have this problem?')

After you have gone through this process it is essential to ask yourself the following questions:

- Do I have the right to try to do something about this?

- Is it wise for me to do something about this?

If the answer to both of these is 'yes' then go for it! If the answer to either question is 'no' then maybe you need to change your own attitude and make the best of the situation. Remember, we need to have the courage to change what we can change, the tolerance to accept what we can't change and the wisdom to know the difference.

Think ahead

You need to plan how you are going to put your feelings across to the other person. Look at the communication principles in Chapter 8 (see pages 85–8) and then do a bit of rehearsing. This may sound rather silly and contrived, but if it is important to you then you are worth it.

Role-play is one useful way to prepare yourself for some future assertive communication. Explain to somebody you trust what it is you are trying to do. Brief them by describing the situation and the person you are going to be dealing with. Give some thought to setting the scene. Where will you be? Will you sit or stand? How are you going to open the conversation so that you have their attention?

Go through the discussion, ensuring that you leave the other person knowing what you would like but remember the importance of listening to them. At the end of the discussion you can ask the person who you have rehearsed with how they thought you came over and what you might do to be even more effective in achieving your goal. Check out what they observed about your body language and your tone of voice.

Another useful tool is a mirror. If you are aware that your body language sometimes lets you down, either because it suggests aggression or passiveness, then a good session in front of a full-length mirror can help. Pretend you are talking to somebody with whom you are trying to behave assertively. Stand with your weight evenly balanced, your shoulders back and head up. Let your arms hang loosely with your hands open and relaxed. Note where you feel any tension and try to relax that part of your body. How do you like yourself when you look assertive? I think you look great! Now's the time to make your assertive statement to express what you would like.

In contrast, adopt a passive pose in front of the mirror and now try putting your point across. Do you notice that your voice has softened and become more hesitant, in keeping with your body posture? You have probably put your weight onto one leg, hunched your shoulders slightly and clasped your hands in front of you. Now adopt an aggressive pose and say the same thing. What has happened to your voice? What is this likely to do to your listener? It will probably cause them to become defensive or to be aggressive back to you, which means it is unlikely to result in a win–win outcome. In this instance you have probably once again put your weight onto one foot, but this time you might be leaning forward slightly; maybe your hands are either on your hips or one is raised and pointing.

Be aware of how these different postures and expressions will look to the other person. What effect will it have on the way they behave towards you; on how seriously they take your comments and how well they listen to you?

Don't forget, you can choose; you don't have to adopt fight or flight but the situation or the person you are dealing with might necessitate moderating your assertiveness either towards the passive or the aggressive end of the spectrum.

Lighten it with laughter

Humour is such a useful vehicle for carrying heavy loads. In the attempt to be assertive it is sometimes easy to fall into a trap of becoming too serious. A bit of humour, a laugh or a smile is really winning and helps diffuse tension. It's also useful to have personal mechanisms for reducing the fear we sometimes feel if we find somebody intimidating or pompous. Not a pretty sight, I know, but just imagine them on the toilet! Angels fly high because they take themselves lightly.

Helping someone else

Unless you are in a position of advocacy – for a child, for a person with special needs, for a member of your staff or for somebody who is officially in your care – you should avoid being assertive on somebody else's behalf. Playing the 'rescuer' role can make you feel good but it reinforces the other person's helplessness, depriving them of an opportunity to choose to be assertive for themselves. It can also be seen as aggressive by the person on the receiving end. By rescuing a 'victim' you are in danger of making somebody else a 'victim' of you.

If you do want to help someone else, I think the best way to do it is to encourage them to be confident. Allow them to rehearse a situation they want to deal with, help them to be clear about what they really want to achieve, help them find a way of expressing themselves. Once again, *listen* to their needs. Telling them what you would do and how you would do it is rarely effective on its own. That person is not you and making it sound easy to deal with stuff could result in them becoming less, not more, confident.

Positive outcomes

In my dealings with assertiveness training, I have encountered numerous 'success stories' of people who have gone through some of the pain to be rewarded with the gain of achieving greater self-respect through a more comfortable relationship with themselves and others. I thought it might be useful to include a few examples of these:

Anna is a graduate in her late twenties whose appearance is very feminine and dainty. Having failed to get any job in her qualified area she attended a series of seminars designed to help people to improve their career prospects through various aspects of jobsearch skills. She had succeeded in getting to the interview stage many times, but was never offered the job. The idea of 'selling herself' filled her with horror as she felt that she didn't want to become 'that sort of person'. She didn't like people who were 'assertive' and neither did her boyfriend. She was clearly unhappy with her life as it was so decided not to close her mind completely during the sessions dealing with assertiveness. After a few weeks she wrote the following: 'My definition of assertiveness is the ability to believe in myself and to be able to communicate a point clearly, precisely and without being pushy or aggressive. It is also a way of being more at peace with myself – feeling that I don't have to validate all of my actions, just being able to explain them clearly if pushed.' Of the next four jobs she was interviewed for, she was offered three.

Helen is a happy, generous woman who likes children and is always willing to help people out. These are nice qualities, except that she often felt stressed and harassed and then guilty for taking it out on her children. She started reading about assertiveness and confidence and began putting some of the skills and ideas into practice. She describes how pleased she felt when her best friend said to her, 'The pity about you becoming more assertive is that I don't feel that I can dump my kids on you now. But I must say that I do like you more!'

John is a quiet, thoughtful man who worked in a busy, changing office environment. He had been suffering stress and was sent for a short series of counselling sessions by his GP. It became clear that, apart from a heavy workload, he was suffering harassment from his predominantly female colleagues. The counsellor helped him to understand more about what was going on and the effect it was having on him. His determination not to let it get the better of him made him learn more about assertiveness. He wrote to the counsellor six months after they had ended their sessions to say that 'I went back into work with my head up and shoulders back. Although I felt like jelly inside I kept my voice steady and controlled. At the first sign of [their] unacceptable behaviour I told them that I wasn't willing to put up with it and that I thought we could improve our working relationship by behaving in a more adult way. Although there was quite a lot of tension in the office for a few days it settled down and we just get on with the work now. It's such a relief not dreading going into work each day, I think I've probably "lightened up" a bit and maybe I'm easier to get along with.'

Congratulations! Now you know that a confident, assertive person is not bossy, selfish, unmasculine, unfeminine, unfriendly or ungenerous, just uncluttered with negative baggage. Enjoy your own success story.

6 Handling conflict

Like death, taxes and change, conflict is an inevitable part of life but it does not have to be synonymous with crisis. It does not necessarily involve entering a danger zone where either you are going to get hurt or you are going to hurt somebody else. Conflict is inevitable; a fight is a choice.

When faced with conflict, it's useful to remember that there doesn't have to be a winner or a loser, what is needed is resolution of the problem. Sadly, because they find conflict so threatening, people tend to avoid it and issues don't become resolved. 'Least said, soonest mended' is a phrase I recently heard from somebody who had been very badly treated in front of a group of colleagues. The person left the situation feeling humiliated and hurt but unwilling to say anything. His explanation: 'Once I let it all out the consequences might be dire.' This is a typical response to conflict situations when we lack confidence. The perception is that the only outcome will be full-scale strife – a dangerous and potentially painful arena to be avoided at all costs. On the other hand, the person who had lashed out at this man was unrepentant and rather self-congratulatory: 'I like to put the cat among the pigeons now and then and get people going, they should speak up for themselves if they don't like it,' he responded. Clearly he wasn't disturbed by the situation and remains comfortable in the 'strife arena' in this relationship.

Exercise

Consider the following questions and decide whether your answer is 'seldom', 'sometimes' or 'frequently':

1. Do you shy away from conflict, seeing it as dangerous and fraught with potential pain?

2. Do you become distressed when you are around people who are arguing or shouting at one another?

3. Can you contradict a domineering person?

4. Do you express your opinions if they differ from those held by others?

5. If you feel someone is being unfair do you say so?

6. If you are interrupted do you make any comment?

If you answered 'frequently' to the first two questions and 'seldom' or 'sometimes' to the others, then it suggests that you see conflict as a danger zone which you would avoid entering. If this is your view of conflict then you probably tend to avoid dealing with contentious issues by either bypassing the people involved, sweeping things under the carpet in the hope that they might go away or even participating in some stamp collecting (see page 49). Does this sound like you? If you appear to go through life avoiding conflict with other people then I suspect that the inner conflict you experience is rather turbulent.

On the other hand, if you answered 'seldom' to the first two questions and 'frequently' to the others then it suggests that you are assertive. A word of caution though, if you have answered this way because you seek out conflict and use it maliciously in order to ensure that you have the upper hand, then you are actually showing a tendency to be aggressive. Is this true of you? If so, then you too probably suffer from inner turbulence. What's it like being alone with yourself in a quiet room? Do you like the person you are with? If you experience that uncomfortable feeling of having to justify yourself and your behaviour it may be a sign that you have behaved badly in a conflict situation.

If you are usually in the middle of these two polarities then it is likely that you generally deal with conflict in an assertive way.

It is important to understand that people have different approaches and attitudes to conflict. Feeling affronted because people don't behave as we think they should can get in the way of moving nearer to understanding the person's point and trying to find a resolution. Sometimes we need to acknowledge to ourselves that we are hurt and then deal with the pain. We need to allow ourselves to feel that pain is often the first step to healing. It is essential to come to terms with the fact that we have to deal with non-assertive behaviour from other people. Remember your rights and have the confidence to assert yourself.

Positive approaches to conflict

Conflict doesn't have to hurt; sometimes it can stimulate change, clear the air and open up new perspectives in a relationship. Too much conformity in groups and families can lead to stagnation, ritual and avoidance of change. We have only one life – to live it in a rut is just a waste. The positive aspects of conflict should not be overlooked in order to maintain a quiet life. Current management thinking advocates conflict as a feature of a learning organisation. Cosy consensus is seen to stifle people and obstruct creativity.

Here are some positive aspects of conflict to bear in mind:

- It lays problems out on the table and opens up discussion.

- It can lead to solutions and a happier outcome for all.

- It increases communication between people and leads to greater mutual understanding.

- It gives the opportunity to explore problems and find creative solutions.

- It releases emotions that have been hidden away.

- It can be great fun making up!

Content and behaviour

There are two aspects to communication: the *content*, what is being said, and the *behaviour*, the way it is being said. Most of the time we are more influenced by the behaviour of the person than by the content of what they are actually saying to us.

Imagine the same lecture being delivered by two different people. The first one walks into the room, sets out his notes and proceeds to read the content in a monotone, making little effort to acknowledge the audience in front of him. The second person walks into the room, scans the audience, makes a warm greeting and delivers the content, varying her voice, pausing at strategic points and creating rapport with the people to whom she is delivering the lecture. Which of the two is likely to succeed in getting the message across? In each case the content is identical but the behaviour will strongly influence the listeners.

Now imagine you have just made a suggestion about a way to tackle something. How would you respond to these two possible responses to your idea?

- 'Well, that idea has its merits, but I'm not sure if it will achieve the outcome we're looking for.'

- 'Oh come on, that's a stupid idea. You know that has no chance of working at all!'

Although the first response is disagreeing with you, you will probably accept the comments and have the confidence to continue to participate in a rational discussion. The second response is likely to result in either your backing down or retaliating aggressively and getting into a battle. In fact, the content is the same in both instances. They are both rejecting your idea, it is the behaviour which is different and it is the behaviour which provokes the response. The most appropriate reply to either of these is something like 'OK, it was just a thought. What's your suggestion?' in a calm, confident tone. If we respond aggressively or passively then we have allowed our response to be determined by the other person's behaviour.

Remember the effect of the parent and child ego state relationships which were outlined in chapter three (see page 21). To deal confidently with conflict we must be influenced by the content of the discussion, not contaminated by the behaviour of the other person or people. That way we remain in control of the situation by avoiding becoming either personally attacked, or attacking the other person in retaliation.

Exercise

Try to observe people in your own social, family or work circles to see how they handle conflict situations. You will start to recognise quite clearly how the response to behaviour can make conflict more difficult to resolve. Television programmes, particularly soaps, are very useful for observing the consequences of behaviour. If you needed an excuse to watch the soaps then you can now put it down to personal development!

When approaching conflict, it's useful to bear in mind the principles of 'content' and 'behaviour'. They'll help you to remain calm and focus on the issue that's at stake, and so make it more likely that you'll work together to reach a solution.

So remember to listen to the content not the behaviour. Concentrate on what is being said, not the way it is being said. You will have a greater understanding of the real issue and be able to assess the importance and merits of what is being discussed. Just because you have become more confident, don't expect the same from everybody. As we have discussed, people might handle a situation of conflict aggressively because inside they feel nervous and uncomfortable about it.

If necessary, discuss the behaviour and the effect it is having. Express how you think somebody's behaviour or attitude might be obscuring the issue and this should help to make you both more aware of the content.

The confident approach to conflict

When a potential conflict situation arises in your life, first of all ask yourself the following questions:

1. What will I gain from avoiding this conflict?

2. What will my personal costs be if I avoid this conflict?

3. What will be the longer-term consequences of 1 and 2?

4. How would I like the long-term picture of my relationship to look in this case?

5. Do I have the right to resolve this conflict situation?

Possible answers might be:

1. The chance to go on feeling aggrieved and thinking I am right and they are wrong.

2. Having to avoid certain subjects and swallow my opinions.

3. The building of a bigger barrier which will prevent us ever really co-operating.

4. Being more relaxed and open, and able to say what I do and don't agree with.

5. Yes, as long as I do it assertively and sensitively.

Working through this process of self-awareness helps to put a clear understanding of the risks of either acting or not acting in any situation. It may result in a decision to do nothing because that is preferable, but at least you will know the consequences and have decided to live with them. If the result is that you do decide to take action – as someone once said, it's better to be a lion for a day than a sheep for all of your life – then here's how to go about it with confidence.

Like all important activities, handling conflict requires planning, so first of all you need to think how best to prepare yourself and how to prepare the environment.

Prepare yourself

Get yourself ready mentally and physically with the following suggestions:

- Ask yourself what outcome you want – be careful what you wish for!

- Try to centre yourself: breathe deeply, be calm. Whatever the situation, be aware that this too will pass.

- Locate your confident self – bring to mind your qualities and capabilities.

- Remember your Bill of Rights (see page 41) – you have the right to be confident and assertive and the right to express yourself.

Prepare the environment

Think about where and when the discussion is going to take place. Remember that you have choices. There might be reasons for not getting into discussion with this person (or this group) at this time, in this place. Consider arranging it for another time or in a different setting, if you think this might help. Sometimes it is easier to say difficult things when you don't have to 'eyeball' the other person; inviting them to walk with you for a while or driving along in a car can be useful tactics to make the situation less tense or embarrassing. People who work with adolescents sometimes find that an effective way of helping them to open up and express themselves is to take them out in a car or get them to help with some physical task. They feel less under pressure to talk than in an office or counselling room situation.

Think about where you'll be physically positioned. If you'll be at a disadvantage, such as sitting while somebody stands over you, then maybe you'll need to stand up and move away to create equal height and comfortable distance. The more you can 'stage-manage' the setting, the more confident, comfortable and in control you will be.

Once you've seen to the preparations it's time to think about what happens during the conflict situation. Here are some techniques and objectives that make for successful conflict resolution.

Broach the issue

When you initiate some discussion that is potentially fraught with conflict it can be helpful to start it with something like, 'I want to say something to you. It is important to me and I've got a lot of feelings about it, so it might not come out very well. Please give me a chance to say what I want to say.'

Active listening

This involves more than just hearing what is being said, or waiting for the other person to finish. First, you need to put yourself in a position where you can hear clearly. Resist the temptation to interrupt; instead focus on the speaker and the content of what they are saying. Show them that you've heard them by repeating main points and clarifying them to check that you have understood.

Express yourself

This means putting forward what you think and, if appropriate, what your feelings are. Letting somebody know your views does not necessarily have to be contentious; telling them how you feel about the issue does not mean making yourself vulnerable. Of course this will depend on the circumstances. It is essential to be in control of your own boundaries (see page 79 for more on boundaries) by choosing how much of your feelings you wish to reveal. But how will they ever know if you don't tell them?

Say what you would like to happen

This will usually be easier to do if you have had time to think it through. I think this is often the trickiest part of conflict; it is harder to actually state what we do want than what we don't want. People are often geared up to express what they are angry or unhappy about, but blow it by being unable to state clearly what they want from the other person.

First we must accept that there is a possibility that we won't get what we want; remember, the other person has rights too. If you are open enough to acknowledge this to yourself then it becomes less of a battle, you are more prepared for a win–win solution. Second, our behaviour must be calm and respectful. This means ensuring that you are taking personal responsibility for what you are saying and acknowledging the other person's rights.

Compromise

I like to think of the following metaphor when it comes to compromise: Build golden bridges over which your enemy can retreat. In order to achieve a win–win outcome to conflict we must be prepared to accept that everybody has certain rights in any situation. If we win and the other person loses then maybe they will become determined to seek revenge some day. On the other hand, if we lose and the other person wins we can develop hostility towards them. Winning the actual issue isn't the only aspect of a situation; retaining your self-respect and respecting the other person is also important. Finding a way that is reasonably agreeable to both parties – some form of workable compromise – is more likely to leave doors open and build positive relationships. However, while compromise is an important aspect of relationships, it is important not to compromise yourself. If you strongly disagree with somebody on the grounds of ethics, morals or principles then you should explain yourself and stay close to what you believe in.

Different people, different approaches

We are all very different, physically, intellectually, emotionally and materially. We tend to find communication easier with people who are similar rather that different to us. This is partly because we feel confident that the other person will understand what we are trying to tell them. As a result of this we behave quite naturally and don't have to put too much thought or preparation into handling conflict with such people. But when dealing with somebody younger or older, more or less articulate, richer or poorer, more or less physically attractive or able-bodied, then we need to make adjustments in our approach and our behaviour.

Exercise

Make a note of the people who you do find it difficult to be in conflict with and those you don't. Now note down situations where you would flee like a lamb from conflict and those where you would stay and fight like a lion.

1. Are there any obvious patterns that emerge here?

2. What can you do to face the situations with more confidence?

Sometimes it is necessary to behave like a lion rather than a lamb.

7 The confidence to say no

I haven't come across many people who don't occasionally find themselves saying yes when they really want to say no. It's great when people are helpful and obliging towards one another, saying yes to a request and meaning it. But there is a price to pay for saying yes when we really mean no. Apart from practical issues of time management or giving away things that belong to us, the big price of not saying no is reduced self-esteem and feelings of anger and resentment. There are situations when people make requests in a manipulative way so that saying no is almost impossible. I recently ran the gauntlet of a line of tin-rattlers all asking me 'Would you like to help disabled children?' What kind of monster does it make me if my answer to this question is a categoric 'No'? I chose not to donate and in this case a qualified 'No, I already have a charity that I regularly support, thank you,' was an appropriate answer for me.

Manipulation can appear in many forms and we must learn to recognise it in order to remain in control rather than be controlled by a manipulative person. Changing your mind is not giving in to manipulation so long as you are choosing. Remember, keeping hold of your own power and responding to people with their 'rights' in mind will help you to stay in control and make the right choices for you and for the situation.

Give some thought now to your own experiences. There may

be some people to whom you find it particularly difficult to say no while with others it is easy.

Consider these examples:

A friend compared to a neighbour

A true 'friend' will respect and accept you whatever you do; you don't need to demonstrate to them that you are generous or obliging. A neighbour, though, might be somebody who doesn't really know you, but you would like to be on good terms with. It is a big risk to cause them to suspect you of meanness or pettiness. So, despite the fact that you always have to go round to 'borrow' your lawnmower back, or spend time cleaning the barbecue before you can use it again, you find yourself saying yes to their request when inside you can hear the screeching echo of no reverberating through your body. This leaves you with negative feelings about the neighbour when in fact it is you who has allowed the situation to happen. Of course, some people will take advantage of us if we let them, but who is to blame? We can't control other people, but we can control ourselves.

Strangers compared to work colleagues

It might be easy to say no to a stranger who is collecting for a charity in which you have no particular interest, but fear of being talked about as 'mean' or 'antisocial' by work colleagues when they're collecting for someone's birthday present can lead you to donate money you really can't afford, even though you hardly know the person whose birthday it is.

Different categories of salespeople

Saying no to a professional salesperson who knocks on your door selling double glazing might be much easier than when it is somebody who you feel sorry for, such as an unemployed person selling dishcloths. In reality, both of those people probably need a 'sale' quite desperately, but you may be less likely to feel guilt saying no to one than to the other.

Exercise

When do you find it easy to say no?

	PERSON	SITUATION
1		
2		
3		

When do you find it difficult to say no?

	PERSON	SITUATION
1		
2		
3		

Think through the differences in your two lists and consider the following questions:

- Is the ability to say no related to power?

- Does it have something to do with guilt?

- Are the relationships involved in your first list more secure?

Go through your second list and in each case try to identify what the difficulty is with regard to saying no. Ask yourself: How do I feel? What might happen if I say no?

Thinking about what might happen if you say no should help you decide whether it's OK to say it or not. Previous chapters have shown that playing the 'nice guy' can lead to all sorts of unhappy repercussions. On the other hand, this book has stressed the importance of choice in situations; you can choose to assert yourself confidently, but sometimes it might not be right for you, or for the situation.

Why is saying no so difficult?

In any dialogue the response is generally much quicker when people say yes rather than no. Take the opportunity to observe some conversations and you are likely to hear more words used when people are refusing than when they are accepting something. This is to do with part of the conventions of language – a 'politeness' that is normal in the usage of English. The word 'yes' is less frequently followed by qualification or explanation than the word 'no'. Try this out – ask people some questions and see what happens. I personally have found this reassuring. People are often anxious about their inability to say no; once you realise that there is a linguistic ritual to refusing requests, you can recognise that it is difficult but that you can learn techniques involved in a mechanical rather than emotional way.

We are conditioned to consider other people. Think about some of the parental messages that you identified in chapter three (see page 23); you were probably rewarded for 'doing as you're told' but reprimanded for refusing. To a child, the words 'Don't you say no to me', spoken in a harsh, authoritative tone, can signify a transitory withdrawal of love from the person we most need to love us. Consequently, even as adults, the very idea of saying no can subconsciously fill us with guilt, dread and foreboding. Remember, this isn't necessarily still relevant to you – the adult – who can rationally decide whether yes or no is an appropriate response to a request from your boss, your neighbour, a member of your family, or somebody rattling a tin in the high street.

Please carry out the following instructions:

1. Put this book down.

2. Lift your chin.

3. Say loudly and clearly, 'No'.

So often people say, 'I just can't say no', or find that they start saying no and it comes out as 'No problem'! Well, you can – you just did. Don't forget that there is a difference between can't and won't. In one case we are in control and choosing, in the other we are suggesting that we are not in control and have no choice. Maybe you didn't follow those instructions. In that case you also said no, so good for you!

How to say no

As the opportunities for saying no are relatively frequent, it's useful to remind yourself of the following every now and then:

- You have the right to say no without feeling guilty.

- It is OK for other people to say no to you.

- Saying yes when you mean no is likely to reduce your confidence.

- It is better to say no at the time than to let somebody down later.

- Saying yes to extra work or obligations might cause you stress.

- Taking on too much might lower your standard of work or mean that the important people in your life don't get their due attention.

- It might not be such a big deal for the other person to get a 'no' response.

- Being respected and respecting yourself is more important than being liked.

As with other techniques of confidence building, particularly assertiveness, practise saying no in relatively uncomplicated situations – something impersonal or casual where you usually just drift into a 'yes'. When it comes to the actual process of saying no, here are some pointers that should help:

- If your instinctive response to something is 'no', hang on to this before 'being nice' takes over – remember what the cost of saying yes might be.

- Be firm but polite.

- Give a reason if you feel it's appropriate, but not an excuse. People can usually see through excuses and they might find it insulting that somebody doesn't respect them enough to be honest with them.

- Buy some thinking time: 'I'll get back to you later'; 'I need to check my diary'.

- Ask for more information: 'How long will it take?'; 'Is there anybody else who could do this for you?' These are also tactics for giving yourself thinking time but beware of taking it on as your problem to find somebody else.

- Use body language and your voice to show that by saying no you are not being hostile but also to demonstrate that you mean what you say and are not going to be manipulated. Stay calm and relaxed – drop your shoulders and breathe deeply so that your voice and pace remains confident, not aggressive or passive. Remember the importance of behaviour in delivering a message (see page 55).

- Think it through. By listening to the other person you might realise that actually you want to say yes after all. Don't be manipulated but it is perfectly all right to change your mind if you are doing so out of choice.

Like most things, with practice saying no becomes easier. You always have a choice but first you must choose whether you want to be choosing!

Setting boundaries

Often situations are not so cut and dried as merely demanding a straight yes or no answer. Imagine that some old friends have telephoned you to say that they intend to visit you over a Bank Holiday weekend. Last time they stayed with you, you felt that they were around for too long, but you really like these people and would love to spend some of the weekend with them. Which of the answers below are you likely to give?

1. 'Yes, great, I'd love to see you.' Then put the phone down and increasingly regret the fact that you have to give a whole weekend over to them. So much so, in fact, that thoughts of your friends bring resentment and tension rather than pleasure.

2. 'Oh, what a shame, I'd love to see you but I've already arranged to go away that weekend.' Then spend the weekend feeling guilty and worrying every time the phone rings, that they might catch you out (or in!).

3. 'Well actually, I'm going to be doing things in the house so I'm not available.' Then feel guilty and also regret not having some time with your friends.

The other option is to state your boundaries clearly. The reply might go something like this: 'It will be nice to see you but I've got a few things I want to do that weekend. How about coming here on Saturday lunchtime and staying until Sunday afternoon?' You have made it clear what you do and don't want, and your friends know where they stand. They can then choose to accept or reject your offer. If they do restate that they want to come for the whole weekend then you can use the 'broken record' technique to repeat what you would like: 'I really would like you to come.

I've got a few other things I want to do, so seeing you from Saturday to Sunday would be great.'

By repeating yourself, using the broken record technique, you reinforce what you do want and make that message clear. Make sure that your head is full of positive thinking while this is going on. Ask yourself:

- Whose home is it? (Yours of course.)

- Whose time is it? (Yours of course.)

- Do I have the right to be respected for what I do or don't want? (I hope, by now, that I don't have to prompt you into a loud yes.)

When your friends do arrive, you are likely to be pleased to see them and delighted to devote your time to their stay. My experience of this has always been that it has strengthened relationships, as people have greater mutual respect and trust when they know where they stand with one another.

Overstepping boundaries

Setting clear boundaries will give people an understanding of what is or isn't acceptable to you. But when people overstep your boundaries it can make you feel used or abused. Some examples of this overstepping are:

- taking advantage of your generosity

- using language or making jokes that are offensive to you

- touching you or encroaching on your physical space

- outstaying a welcome.

You may be able to think of situations where something has gone too far and you have felt angry, upset or uncomfortable about it but haven't had the confidence to say so.

It is important to respect other people's boundaries. If you are not sure what they are, find out. Ask them what it is they would like from you and how they want to be treated. Sometimes we are prevented from offering kindness to people because we are inhibited by not knowing how to do that. When people have suffered bereavement or sadness in their life they often find themselves being avoided as if they were contagious. The explanation is usually that people don't know what to say. Of course this comes from a lack of confidence but my response to this is to ask the person whether they want to talk about it. How would they like you to treat them? Is it better if you do or don't mention the person they have lost? By doing this you give the grieving person the opportunity to state their boundaries and you are able to behave in a way that respects those boundaries without the person feeling isolated and alone with their grief. This will give that person more confidence in themselves and in you.

Here are a few examples of some typical boundaries that might exist in relation to certain aspects of life:

SITUATION / RELATIONSHIP	BOUNDARIES
Work	Willing to give all when I'm there but not to take work home or stay after 6 p.m. unless very special circumstances.
Home	Want a reasonable standard of tidiness and order in the house.
Friends	Will give help but not expect to be 'dumped' on.

Other examples of boundaries might occur around possessions, family, hobbies, sex, children, neighbours, privacy and religion.

Exercise

Now think about different aspects and relationships in your life. What are your boundaries – what do you choose to protect?

	SITUATION / RELATIONSHIP	BOUNDARIES
1		
2		
3		
4		
5		

Now that you are clear about your own boundaries you can give some thought to how you will confidently explain those boundaries to people who need to be more aware of them. The following chapter (see page 84) on communication will help you with this.

Please don't confuse this talk about saying no with being selfish, unco-operative and mean. Generosity, helpfulness, kindness and sharing are all traits that people who are truly confident possess in abundance.

Remember that saying yes to something you don't want to do damages your confidence, but saying yes to something you do want to do is an opportunity to do it joyfully and confidently.

8 Clear communication

It will have become increasingly clear to you how important communication is to feeling confident and also to being seen as confident. One thing that defines us as humans is our ability to communicate. As we grow and develop, so do our communication skills. This chapter deals with principles and techniques of confident, effective communication. In the words of John Donne, 'No man is an island, entire unto himself.' However gregarious or private we are as individuals, we do have to communicate with other people. Just because we have learned language doesn't mean that we are good at expressing ourselves, and not being able to do so can leave us feeling frustrated and lacking in confidence.

Poor communication skills always emerge as one of the main concerns of employers in recruiting good people. After technical/practical requirements, the two most sought after skills are communication and customer service. This applies at all levels, in all industries and organisations. Have you ever tried to get information from somebody who is technically brilliant but can't communicate at a level that will achieve everybody's needs? Similarly, however creative somebody is, if they are not able to translate their ideas so that other people can appreciate them then they will fail. It is taken for granted that communication is common sense. Well, maybe, but my view then is that common sense is not very common. Besides, my common sense, gleaned predominantly from my parent ego state, might fundamentally differ from yours.

Communication is complex

In every dialogue between you and me there is:

- The person I think I am.

- The person you think I am.

- The person I think you think I am.

- The person you think I think you are . . . (OK, I'll stop there!)

But just consider how little notice you take of somebody you regard as insignificant, compared to somebody you see as powerful? On the other hand, how effective are you in communicating with somebody you think is not impressed by or interested in what you have to say?

I'd like to introduce you to five principles to help you communicate effectively:

Be direct

If there is something to be said then don't pussy-foot around, get on and say it. Avoid the tendency to use preambles like, 'I know you're really busy but . . .', 'I'm ever so sorry to trouble you . . .', 'You'll probably think I'm awful saying this . . .' These give the other person the opportunity to anticipate what we might be going to say, encouraging them to adopt a defensive or dismissive attitude. It is far more effective to directly state what we are trying to put across to somebody. That doesn't mean that we have to be rude, abrupt or unpleasant. It merely means that we give the impression of having confidently considered what we want to communicate before launching into sound. This gains respect and prevents clouding the message.

Be appropriate

Communication is most successful when the 'sender' is sensitive to the 'receiver'. I am not advocating that we should change our style of communicating to suit who we are with, but a degree of sensitivity to the other person will help. If you are making a point to your boss then your style might be different from that of criticising your partner or trying to be persuasive to a child. Not only the person, but the time and place should be considered.

Take responsibility

'I think . . .', 'In my opinion . . .', 'My understanding is . . .' are all far more effective ways of putting across our view than 'You are . . .', 'That's not right . . .' or 'It isn't like that . . .' We have the right to our opinions but ours is not the only opinion. People will be far more receptive to being told things about themselves if it is offered as your opinion rather than a universal statement.

Think about the effect these statements might have:

1. 'Your driving is terrible.'

2. 'That outfit doesn't suit you.'

3. 'You can't say that.'

4. 'You never clean the bath out/empty the dishwasher/lock up the office properly.'

5. 'You were horrible to me last night.'

6. 'That won't work, you should do it like this.'

The responses to each of these are likely to be defensive or confrontational. They are all put-downs and are causes of lack of confidence. On the other hand, taking ownership of what you are saying will result in the other person being less threatened and more amenable to listening to you.

Here are some confident alternatives:

1. 'I think you drive too fast sometimes/I don't always feel very confident driving with you.'

2. 'I'm not sure that I'm keen on that outfit on you.'

3. 'I don't agree with what you are saying.'

4. 'I would like to explain the way I like the bath to be cleaned/the dishwasher emptied/the office locked up.'

5. 'I was upset about the way I felt you were treating me last night.'

6. 'I would approach that differently, have you thought about doing it this way?'

These approaches will not be seen as a put-down, nor as 'nagging' and so people will be more attuned to listen to your view. That will result in you having more self-confidence and in the other person having more confidence in continuing the discussion.

Remain calm and in control

It is difficult to look confident when your shoulders are hunched right up to your earlobes, your fists are clenched and your face is red. Taking deep breaths and letting some of the obvious tension drain from you will help. Communicating confidently spontaneously can be more difficult than when we've had time to prepare what we want to say. But a few seconds spent taking control of emotions will ensure that your brain is in gear before your tongue starts working. By controlling the tone and volume of your voice you can make the message less emotional. By ensuring that your body is relaxed and in tune with the words you are saying you become more plausible.

Be willing to listen

The most overlooked aspect of communication is listening. People often think that confident communication skills are about being articulate, telling a good tale or having a wide vocabulary. Yes, all of these are important, but the ability and willingness to listen to others is more important. We tend to fall into the category of either listening distractedly, allowing other things, whether in our head or around us, to interfere, or dismissively, filtering only the bits we want to take in. When we are listening to somebody we need to suspend judgement and emotion until we have heard them out and understood. Listening to the other person's point of view is as important as expressing our own view of a situation. 'But that looks as if you are weak and going to give in to the other person,' some might say. This is not actually the case. When we are listening to somebody, as well as putting across our own view, we are actually more in control and therefore more assertive because we are really focused.

Exercise

Consider these questions about your own listening skills and tick the answers that are relevant to you.

While the other person is talking, do you:

	OFTEN	SOMETIMES	NEVER
Rehearse what you are going to say?			
Wish they would get to the point more quickly?			
Interrupt?			
Mind-read?			
Judge them by appearance or accent?			
Filter what you already think or want to think?			
Daydream?			

Most of us do some of these some of the time. We might think we are listening but we're not. When we communicate confidently we respect the other person's right to put their views across. They can't do this if we are not listening to them.

In reality not listening is more complicated than 'just' not doing it. As the questionnaire demonstrates, what actually happens is that we think we are listening but more often than not we are listening to what we think we are hearing rather than what is being said. People whose profession is to listen have spent years being trained to do so. It is a very difficult skill to achieve mastery in. In a recorded counselling or therapy situation it is likely that the voice of the listener will only be heard for 10 per cent of the 50 minutes. The benefit to people of being able to just talk can be amazing. On the other hand, if you tape normal, everyday conversation you will hear a 'my go' – 'your go' pattern. It might be something like this. 'Did you have a good weekend?' 'Yeah it was great we went down to the coast. It was a lovely day.' 'Oh we just stayed home and did the garden.' Normal, natural and perfectly acceptable. But can you see that there is no real listening here? A real listening response to 'We went down to the coast, it was a lovely day,' would be, 'That sounds nice. Where did you go, what did you do?' Real listening doesn't involve capturing the subject and making it your own, it involves enabling the other person to continue in order that they can express more.

A word of warning: I am not suggesting that we should pursue 'real' listening all the time. We would never get through the day. The conversation I illustrated is normal social interaction. What I am drawing attention to is that when we need to assert ourselves it is necessary to really listen in order to maximise our under-standing and make the appropriate response. I would say that the workshop I run that empowers people most is that on listening. By really listening to what is said, we can understand and gain control of a situation and communicate with a confidence based on really knowing what is going on in a situation.

There used to be a billboard advertisement for a charity concerned with children. It was a picture of a scruffy, spotty, unsmiling teenage boy. The caption said 'What he needs is a damned good listening to.' I still find this very powerful as a reminder that if we want somebody to behave differently then the starting point is to find out why they behave like they do. This is very relevant to managing people, bringing up children and enjoying healthy personal relationships.

'It's the way she said it'

I'm sure you can relate to a time when you have been upset, angered or confused by how something has been said to you rather than what has been said. In many of the examples in this book you may have felt strong disagreement with what I have proposed as 'model' statements. Yes, I understand that completely because you are not able to hear my tone of voice as I would actually speak them.

Research tells us that the effectiveness of communication relies 7 per cent on words, 35 per cent on tone of voice and 58 per cent on body language. The statistics relate to face-to-face communication but are still relevant to other media even though the numbers may change. Think about receiving a letter: the envelope it arrives in, the quality of the paper, the layout and the importance of the signature will all precede the actual content in influencing your initial impression and consequently the letter's effectiveness in achieving its objective. These judgements are likely to be subconscious; we will not be aware of making them. So, that was just a letter. Imagine how much more complex our subconscious responses are to flesh and blood. Except of course it rarely is flesh and blood, unless you work in a casualty ward or a massage parlour.

Tone of voice

Clarity, pitch – high or low – pace, accent, warmth and volume will all have an impact on your communication. If you mumble people won't bother to listen. If you shout and accentuate words emphatically then people may not bother to listen to you. Again, it's important to consider what you are trying to get across and then controlling your voice. If you are responsible for getting people out of a building that is on fire then authority and urgency is essential. If you are trying to persuade somebody to agree with you then a calm, friendly tone of voice might be more appropriate.

Exercise

Take a simple question, 'Who exactly do you mean?' and say it out loud in a variety of ways.

You will hear that it can sound aggressive, defensive, sarcastic or gossipy. The intonation you use will affect the response you get.

Silent communicators

Facial expression, posture, grooming and eye contact are just some of the factors that communicate information to us before somebody even opens their mouth to speak. Some people are antagonistic to the notion that body language is important because they have a strong sense that you should take people as they are and not make judgements. Well, yes, I am in agreement with this, but the reality is that we don't know what people are, we can only take them as we perceive them to be.

If somebody is smiling, with a relaxed, confident posture, is appropriately clean with an inoffensive odour, makes comfortable eye contact and is standing or sitting at the right distance from me, then I am likely to subconsciously feel at ease and happy to listen to what they have to say. If, however, the opposite is true in one or two points, then my subconscious 'judgement' will be affecting how I receive what they have to say. The effect of my judgement in this case may trigger a negative response towards the person and therefore obscure whatever they proceed to communicate. I will not necessarily appreciate what they think or feel because I may have interpreted their communication from my own perception of them.

So what can we do about this? How can we try to ensure that other people like what they see and hear when we communicate?

What others see

Although we can't control how other people perceive us we can take responsibility for how we present ourselves. We have the opportunity to ask 'What do I want this person/these people to see when I am trying to communicate my message?' If the answer is 'a confident communicator' then it is up to you to ensure that is what they will be looking at.

Facial expression

This should be appropriate to the subject. A smile is winning, disarming and can put people at ease, but is not appropriate in all communication. Empathy with the situation, the subject and the receiver will help you to determine the appropriate facial expression. I have witnessed people trying to deliver good customer service and being told 'You can wipe that grin off your face' by their customer! Similarly, if you are delivering bad news or saying something you feel serious about, your message might not be properly understood if you are saying it with a smile. These mixed messages get us into trouble; telling somebody you don't like their behaviour but smiling as you do so gives them permission to continue behaving that way with you.

Posture

Your posture will communicate confidence, energy and personal control if you get it right. As we have seen in earlier chapters, head up with relaxed shoulders and an open stance will demonstrate a command of yourself and the situation.

Grooming and general appearance

Personal hygiene is fundamental; we can't wait to get away from people who don't smell very nice, however convincing their spoken message may be. Appearance in general is another one of those thorny issues that people argue about. Personally, I advocate a dress code at work. It eliminates inappropriate dress and establishes a corporate, businesslike ethos which can be interpreted in a way that is appropriate to the industry or organisation's aims. People argue that it goes against individuality, self-expression and people's rights. I see their point but this is another issue where common sense isn't necessarily common and I've observed many situations where inappropriate dress in the workplace has got in the way of good communication because the 'sender' of a message has not been taken seriously by the 'receiver'.

Look organised

Whether it's your desk, your bag or your papers, anything that can be seen will have an influence on the effectiveness of your communication. People have far more confidence when dealing with somebody who looks as though they've got their finger on the button. Take some time to organise your paperwork so that you don't have to keep somebody waiting while you search for a document or some notes. This applies to work and personal situations and is particularly relevant if you are dealing with money matters.

Eye contact

Comfortable eye contact demonstrates respect and straight-forwardness. When we describe somebody as 'a bit shifty' it is usually because they have avoided our eye. On the other hand, a stare can feel very aggressive. If you find it difficult to make eye contact with somebody, try focusing on the bridge of their nose. After a while, if you are communicating well and listening genuinely you will forget about it and eye contact will become easy and natural. When people are thinking and remembering things, they will look away from you before they make a response. This is normal and natural, not an avoidance of eye contact.

Proximity

How close you are to another person will have an effect on how they receive your communication. If you step into somebody's space they may feel threatened by you and see it as aggressive. The response may then be that they become aggressive or that they back off passively. Confident communicators want to maintain an assertive dialogue so it is important to be sensitive to other people's space. The cultural norm for Northern Europeans is just short of arm's length. If you look around, you will see that most business or formal communication is conducted at this distance. Be aware though that this isn't necessarily the cultural norm for everybody. In many cultures people are comfortable being a lot closer. They are not being offensive, this is merely a different norm. If you feel uncomfortable then step back a little, maintaining eye contact and a positive regard toward that person.

Create rapport

In all communication, creating rapport with the other person will enable you to quickly get on to each other's wavelength and increase the effectiveness of what is being said and heard. Rapport creates trust and understanding between people. We have greater confidence in people we can relate to; people who use similar language, have similar views and in some cases who look similar to us. If the general dress code for a meeting is suits or smart business wear then people will be more likely to listen to what you say if you too are dressed that way. On the other hand, I know lots of people who do manual work and wear clothes appropriate to that work. They admit to responding more favourably to a 'dressed down' manager giving them instructions than to somebody who looks like she or he is going to a board meeting. Clothes are just one aspect of rapport, others involve pace, tone, vocabulary of speech and positioning of body. Next time you are in a pub or a café look around at people. You will start to notice that where two people are engaged in congenial conversation they adopt a similar body posture to one another. They are truly in rapport, relating to one another on the same level.

Exercise

Choose a situation where you are in one-to-one discussion with somebody and observe their body language and then see if yours matches. This includes the way you are sitting, the angle of your head, your facial expressions and whether or not your arms are folded.

If you are not matched then just slowly change some of your own posture so that it mirrors the other person. What about your voice? Try to make it similar in tone and pace to the other person. You will find that they become more relaxed with you, have more confidence in talking to you and that you too will start to feel more confident with them.

Communicating via technology

We have considered the concept of 'silent communicators' in terms of non-verbal communication but of course there is also the whole issue of communicating in writing. We don't have the advantage of being able to observe the response to written communication or to immediately clarify, pacify or expand on what we have said in a letter, email or text. The written word can also be held as evidence or proof and needs consideration. Put yourself in the shoes of the receiver; will your message help or hinder a situation or a relationship? You are only able to read the words on these pages, you don't have the added information that tone of voice and body language of the writer would give you. It's really important to bear this in mind when sending a message, by whatever medium.

To text or not to text

Research tells us that men now declare their love in words far more than before. The medium? Text messaging. This is great and I'm all for it, but the downside of this ingenious technology is that people are able to – and do – send messages that they perhaps wouldn't express if they waited until the morning, or until the emotion of a situation had subsided. When we lack confidence to express ourselves it is very easy to hide behind the seemingly safe distance of a text message. Before sending off your message, just ask yourself: Would I say this to the person if they were standing in front of me? How will the recipient feel when they read this message?

Email etiquette

Bear in mind that when your message appears in somebody's inbox it may be far lower on their priority list than it is on yours. In this case, it might not be the most effective method of communicating if it is an urgent matter for you.

How do your emails look to the receiver? I am amazed at the number of people who would never send out a letter, a report or even a greetings card that wasn't accurate in spelling and grammar, yet their emails are full of errors. This serves to undermine the message and therefore will interfere with the objective.

Be aware of CAPITAL LETTERS. They are the visual equivalent of shouting and as we have seen in earlier chapters, nobody really responds well to being shouted at.

Keep safe

Just a word about situations of potential danger. If you are in doubt about a person with regard to your personal safety, then there is no doubt. Protect yourself by removing yourself from the situation. This book is about confidence. It will help you to deal effectively with different people and different situations. However, it is not about becoming so confident that you ignore your intuition and put yourself into, or remain in, situations that your gut reaction tells you are dangerous.

Steps to confident communication

- Know what you want to achieve/what your objective is.

- Choose the appropriate method – face-to-face, telephone, letter, email, words, pictures. Which will best achieve your objective?

- Choose the right time and place.

- Gain attention.

- Establish and maintain an open relationship.

- Actively listen, appreciate and understand the other person's viewpoint.

- Be clear, brief and coherent.

- Choose how you want to be seen and dress accordingly and appropriately.

- Control your non-verbal messages and read those of your receiver/s.

- Create a rapport with the person/people you are talking to.

Part three

Confidence in the real world

9   Confidence at work

The workplace can be a minefield of challenges for people who lack confidence. We have to deal with managers, employees, colleagues and customers **and** get the work done. I never cease to be amazed at how many people who do difficult jobs well confess to lacking in confidence. I often hear people say to a colleague, 'You don't lack confidence, you always look so in control and capable'. Well, this might be how people see you. As we said in the beginning, confidence is not just what we feel but also what we project. You are what you are but you are also what other people think you are. If you are told by people that they perceive you as confident allow that to wash through you and accept it. Never mind the 'Yes, but they don't know'; think of the swan.

There is no doubt that you get better treatment from people when they have confidence in you, be they colleagues or customers. A positive attitude usually helps you to make great strides in gaining people's confidence. Attitude influences behaviour so take a moment to compare the difference between positive and negative:

NEGATIVE	POSITIVE
unco-operative	interested
cynical	respectful

NEGATIVE	POSITIVE
defensive	friendly
miserable	optimistic
aloof	energetic

Which of these characteristics do you want to be working along-side? We really are in charge of choosing how we behave. If you lack confidence then that is a problem that you have to deal with, and the fact that you are reading this means you probably are dealing with it. But it is not acceptable to pollute your workplace because of your own issues. Choosing to behave positively will influence how others behave towards you. What you give will affect what you get and if you express energy, interest, respect, friend-liness and optimism in your workplace then you are likely to get back the same from colleagues and customers. Of course there will always be 'difficult people' to deal with and you need strategies to help you do this confidently.

Sometimes it's not easy to be positive, we all have days when we feel below par or when we have problems on our mind. This, like many other of life's challenges, involves maintaining a balance of taking care to protect yourself and putting on a brave face to get you through the day. In a team of ten colleagues, the chances are that two of them might be going through some kind of life crisis. A caring, sensitive boss and a supportive team culture can help with this but we can't allow it to take over. Sometimes being able to park your personal problems and throw yourself into the distractions of the working day can help. In the same way as you might check your appearance in a mirror as you pass it, get into the habit of checking your attitude. Choosing to be positive will win you friendship, support and respect, all of which help the working day to go by less painfully.

I mentioned 'difficult people'; I personally prefer to think of it as difficult situations rather than people. I fear that once we label somebody as difficult we are almost giving ourselves permission to not get on with them. Of course if you don't have to get on with somebody then that's fine. I'm a strong believer in avoiding people who I don't enjoy being around and who can, if I allow them, sap my energy and leave me feeling negative. In work though, we usually don't have the luxury of choosing the people around us.

Dealing with angry customers

The skills outlined in chapter eleven (see page 129) for being a confident consumer will transfer to dealing with customers as well as to being one. Respect, fairness, firmness and attentive listening, accompanied by a positive attitude, will all help you to feel confident and help others to have confidence in you. Sometimes, though, the job requires you to gear up your responses. When people are angry:

- Remain as calm as possible. If you're not in control of yourself then the other person will start controlling you. Do an 'Emergency Stop' – take a deep breath and put positive words into your head.

- Hear the person out. Don't attempt to manage an angry person until you have allowed them to let off steam. A barking dog can't bite.

- Listen to what the other person is saying before attempting to sort out the issue – remember your perception of what they want may be different from theirs. Put yourself in their shoes.

- Use positive, calming body language and breathe! Don't look like you're up for a fight.

- Speak slowly and maintain self-control. Control the situation not the person.

- Always look for a good outcome to the situation rather than attempting to sort someone's attitude out. Once you start trying to win, you have lost.

- Don't take it personally. It just happens that it is you there in front of them, or on the telephone to them. It's your job.

- If you feel yourself becoming angry, increase your distance. If necessary remove yourself from the situation. They can only get your goat if they know where it is tethered!

I frequently encounter people who have no problem in asserting confidence when dealing with customers but are unable to do the same with colleagues, bosses or members of staff. If this is your experience then try working out exactly what you do when you are dealing with a difficult customer and transfer the skill you use into a colleague situation. It is often helpful to practise saying things that need to be said, ideally with a sensitive, supportive colleague.

Get yourself a mentor

It is so useful to have somebody experienced who you can trust to advise you, listen to you and guide you. Somebody who has been around the company for a while who under-stands the culture and the norms will help you get things in perspective and think through how you can best deal with situations that arise.

Dealing with bullies

Sadly, bullying at work is not uncommon but it often goes on unchallenged. Often people leave their job because of it without having tackled the situation. This is not the person's fault. It takes enormous courage to confront bullying; the culture in some organisations is such that people can report a situation of bullying without fear of reprisal but I regret to say that this is the exception. In any bullying situation there are three players: the person who is being bullied, the person who is doing the bullying and the people around who, by lack of action, allow it to go on.

If you feel you are a victim of bullying, be kind to yourself and start taking steps to change things. First, have a bit of compassion for yourself. It's a horrible thing to be happening to you but it doesn't mean that you are inadequate. Believe me, very skilled, personable, competent people undergo situations of bullying and it has a hugely undermining effect on their confidence. You are not to blame, but you are the person who can choose to do something about it. The path of least resistance rarely leads to happiness. Leaving your job may be your preferred option, and that's fine if it is your choice, but doing so when it doesn't suit you should be a last resort. Bullying can make people ill; it can seriously erode your self-esteem. By taking action you can start to restore that self-esteem and escape from the role of victim.

Write it down

Start and maintain a log of all situations and conversations where you feel that bullying is taking place. People who bully can be extremely subtle, so much so that you can be left doubting your judgement and even feeling guilty. Write down the date, the place, the situation and the words spoken. Once you start to do this you will recognise a pattern of behaviour and it will give you the confidence to tackle it.

Confronting the bully

In order to do this it will help if you are clear about several things:

- what is actually being done/said to you

- how it makes you feel/behave

- what changes you want to see

- how things would be if the situation stopped.

By working through these questions you will gain more confidence to confront the person. However, before doing so, you need to rehearse your words and think about what has been written in chapters five and eight on assertiveness and communication (see pages 54 and 84). Ask yourself, 'Do I have the right to confront this person?' and if the answer is 'yes', which, if you are being bullied is certainly so, lift your head up, put your shoulders back, breathe and do it.

Reporting the bully

I would never accuse anybody who couldn't confront a bully of being a coward. The sheer nature of the situation makes it impossible for some people. You do, however, have the right not to be bullied and the right to ask for help. The log you have kept will be immensely important in seeking help. You should be able to do so from an HR department, from a senior person in the organisation or from a Trade Union representative. A word of caution here: sometimes people are just rubbish at dealing with this issue even though they have the responsibility to do so. If this is the case, it's not your fault. If you have a valid grievance, don't let them undermine your confidence in being determined to resolve the problem. Confiding in a colleague you trust will help to boost your confidence and maybe give you the opportunity to practise what you will say.

Changing bullying behaviour

If somebody has been identified as a bully then an organisation has a responsibility to help that person to develop their interpersonal skills in order that they no longer use such tactics. Bullying can be a symptom of lack of confidence even though it looks quite the opposite.

Communication at work

'The problem in this place is lack of communication.' I would be a rich woman if I had collected money every time I heard somebody say that. Have you ever said it? If so, what did you really mean? You weren't being told enough? The grapevine was stronger than formal channels of communication? Or maybe you just weren't being told what you wanted to hear? My first response to this is always 'What do you want to know and what is the best way of trying to find out?'

Hiding places

In work and personal situations people complaining about lack of communication can be one of those 'hiding places' that people use as an excuse for not dealing assertively with an issue. You can recognise these hiding places by the use of abstract words: '*Management* never trust us'; '*Relationships* have been soured'; '*The company* keep us in the dark'; '*Communication* has broken down'. Another way of recognising hiding places is by use of absolute terms: '*Nobody* listens to me'; 'I *always* get blamed'. You probably have your own examples and can start to recognise that there is an element of 'victim' in all this where the person opts out of taking responsibility because things are 'being done to them'.

Make your messages powerful

I am not saying that issues that people are concerned about when they use such terms have no importance; of course they have. What I am saying is that when we use vague, unclear messages, we give people the opportunity to dismiss what we are saying and ignore our grumbles. If you recognise that you sometimes are a sender of indirect language then I suggest you refer back to the five principles of confident communication in chapter eight (pages 85–8), use what you have learned about assertive communication in order to express your concerns and see how much more powerfully it will be received.

Thinking through what your issues really are will give you the opportunity to ask yourself whether they are important enough for you to do something about them. If the answer to this is no then get over yourself, change your negative thoughts into positive ones and get on with the job. If the answer is yes, do some preparation on how you will approach the issue and with whom. Moaning is an unattractive, negative time-waster; it reduces our self-esteem and the esteem of others. Confident people deal with what needs to be dealt with in order to free up their spirit to tackle the day positively.

Influencing skills

In order to influence we need to have power. Your reaction may be that this counts you out if you don't see yourself in a position of power, but it doesn't necessarily mean high status, social or business muscle. There are many sources of power and they change in different situations. Think of an office junior working in a place where a new technology has recently been introduced. That young person may have far better IT skills than his or her colleagues, giving them the confidence to assert themselves and have influence in that situation. Another example is somebody who, regardless of their status, has really good interpersonal skills. People will listen to this person and be influenced by what they have to say.

Conventional status is an obvious form of power. The hirer and firer in an organisation holds authority, but not necessarily the influence that motivates people to do a good job, take pride in their work and continually seek to improve. Influencing is far more subtle than just holding power. It is about persuading people to your point of view in order that they act or respond in the way you want them to. I choose persuading rather than advising. I have come to the conclusion that unsolicited advice wastes valuable breath. If it worked then none of us would ever be overweight, unfit, hungover or guilty of speeding. Advice is issued to us all the time, but we are not necessarily influenced by it.

This is another instance when a win–win outcome will achieve the best goal. Effective influencing requires a respect for the person/people we want to influence, not manipulation. When you want or need to influence people, starting off with effective questioning will help to involve the other person.

We often assume that other people are motivated by the same things we are motivated by. This isn't true, so therefore they will not necessarily be influenced by the same things we are. When we influence people successfully it is because we have convinced them of the benefits of doing something. Discovering what is important to somebody, what their values are and what motivates them helps us to plan how best we can influence them.

I have recently been working with an organisation undergoing a lot of change: nothing new there of course. But what was refreshing was the ease with which the change evolved. The company spent a lot of time understanding the values of its employees: what was important to them in their jobs and therefore what motivated them. As you would expect, salary was high on the list, but so was pride in the product, teamwork and opportunities to be creative. With this understanding, the company was able to introduce change in a way that was acceptable to people because they were able to see the benefit of it.

The power of listening

The example I have just given can only happen if people have developed their skills in listening. As we have seen throughout this book, listening is essential to confident communication. In his excellent book *Seven Skills of Highly Effective People*, Peter Covey uses the phrase 'seek first to understand, then to be understood'. This is the opposite to how we usually do things. It is more common to take the 'what you need to understand' approach. We try to implant what we want somebody to know without first hearing their perspective. By listening to somebody, you can learn what they actually think, feel and want, i.e. what is of value to them. This then gives the opportunity to express what you want in terms that will be acceptable to them.

Making requests at work

Asking people to do things isn't always easy. People often admit to doing everything themselves because it is easier than plucking up the confidence to ask somebody to perform a task, even when it is part of the other person's job. This results in stress through having too much to do and lack of self-esteem because we feel stupid for having opted out of asking for what we want. The following pointers will help you make requests confidently and assertively:

- Decide exactly what it is you want:

  - The standard, e.g. a beautifully bound report or bullet points on an email

  - Timing – when you need it by, how long you expect it to take

  - The full picture – where it fits into the goals and how it will be used.

- Work out in your mind a clear and concise statement:

  - Use a 'script' if necessary to ensure you know exactly what you are asking for

  - Rehearse positive self-talk: 'I have the right to ask for this'

  - Remember others have rights and be prepared to negotiate

- Ensure you have the person's attention before you proceed:

  - Check their body language and readiness to hear you

  - Check any tension of your own.

- Deliver your statement going directly to the point:

  - Don't apologise unnecessarily

  - Don't put yourself down

  - Do keep your message clear

  - Do check that they understand what it is you want.

Let's imagine that you feel you are entitled to a pay rise and have decided to discuss this with your line manager. An effective way of communicating your request would go something like this:

> *Thanks for taking the time to see me, Jane. As you are aware, I've taken on some new responsibilities in the past year and I think that this warrants a salary review. I've done some research and the job I'm currently doing has a market value of £x. We established during my annual appraisal that the company is happy with my performance and so I am asking for a salary increase of £x to be effective from [date].*

A manager's role

If you are employed to manage, lead or supervise people then you have the responsibility to do so confidently. I was recently involved in a situation where the relationships in an office had become so dysfunctional that they were posing a threat to the business. Gary came into the department as manager two years ago. He was a creative, brilliant marketer with an easy-going and friendly personality. Most people in the team were committed and motivated but there was one person whose personal life was always more important than her job. She started to take advantage of Gary's lack of supervision and got away with a lot, including taking extra holiday days which she was not recording and he didn't check. As you can imagine, other people in the team were pretty fed up with their colleague but also frustrated with Gary for allowing it to happen. His attitude was that he was busy dealing with important things and needed to be able to trust people to do the right thing. He had confidence in his staff but in one case it was a false, untested confidence.

Imagine a scale of management style with 'participative' at one end and 'authoritarian' at the other. Most people, when asked, say that they prefer to be at the participative end, involving people in decisions and trusting them to perform well. When I then ask where their manager is on the scale they usually respond that their manager is further towards the authoritarian end. The discussion will usually take the direction of accepting that authoritarian is effective as long as it is done 'nicely'. What people are really meaning is that it is right that people with authority use that authority so long as their behaviour is consistent, fair, honest and respectful.

The result of the situation in Gary's case was that his lack of assertiveness tipped the balance of power. When he realised this he became extremely agitated and there was a public showdown. It took outside help to get people working effectively back together and the cost to the business was high. It would not have happened if Gary had laid down the rules, a notion which is unpalatable to people who claim to dislike an authoritarian approach to managing people.

Rules

Clear rules benefit both employers and employees. They set standards of conduct at work and make clear to people what is expected of them. A disciplinary procedure is not about sacking people. It is a way of professionally ensuring that standards of conduct and performance are met. On occasions situations of gross misconduct will lead to warnings or instant dismissal but mostly the situation of discipline is not over a dramatic incident. It is more like Gary's situation where there was a need for behaviour to be 'nipped in the bud'. Unfortunately though, many managers, like Gary, shy away from this and once the bud has bloomed it is far more difficult to deal with discreetly and constructively.

Discipline at work will be effective if we:

- make sure people know what the rules are

- refer to the rules whenever necessary

- negotiate changes to rules where appropriate

- apply the discipline regime consistently and fairly.

Are you familiar with your company's disciplinary procedure? I am frequently surprised how few managers answer yes to this question. It is likely that people in your HR department have spent a lot of time and money putting together your company's procedure. Locate it, read it, use it and ask for help in interpreting it. In the majority of cases you will not need to take formal action. Assertive discussions with your staff can ensure that discipline is maintained and encourage self-discipline in them.

ACAS (Advisory, Conciliation and Arbitration Service) publish an excellent handbook on discipline at work. It will be useful to you whatever the size of your organisation. (See the Quick Reference section on page 163 for contact details.)

Be positive

In chapter eight we talked about the importance of communication and of positive behaviour (see page 84). What we communicate is what we are and what we think. It is important to look the business. Present yourself well, think about how you want people to see you and what will achieve your goals. You need to look as though you are in control, comfortable with your surroundings, efficient and organised. You will have more confidence in yourself if this is how you present yourself. Equally important is the fact that others will also have confidence in you through the way you look.

We also impart confidence by the way we sound, particularly the words we choose. Taking control of situations and expressing ourselves positively gives more power. If we take responsibility for the language we use then we exercise more control over a situation. Other people don't control us unless we allow them to. Consider the following statement:

> 'Now you've made me late for the meeting, they'll all think I'm incompetent and they'll make me nervous.'

What has really happened is that this person has allowed somebody else to overstay their welcome or waste their time. They know it won't look professional when they turn up late at their meeting and their confidence will be undermined. But they are trying to blame somebody else when actually they need to take responsibility for what has happened.

Whether we like it or not work is a grown-up arena. The adult ego state is generally the one to be adopted during our working hours. Hopefully your work culture allows some free child activities in between the serious stuff: good colleague relationships, good coffee, social opportunities, etc. But it is important to take responsibility for being a positive employee and a positive colleague, having the confidence to adapt your behaviour to what is required.

10 Confidence at home

It is a paradox that the people we love and who love us sometimes cause us the greatest problems. Difficult situations at work can cause a reluctance to get out of bed, a tendency to wish the week away and a lot of daydreaming about winning the lottery. At worst, they cause anxiety and stress. Usually though, work situations can be dealt with and a good weekend or a holiday put them all in perspective. I believe that we should do our best at work, develop skills to be competent at the job and have a positive, co-operative attitude. I also, however, believe in having a healthy 'sod it' factor in order to keep things in proportion and ensure a healthy, balanced life.

When things are wrong in our personal life though, they tend to hit us far more profoundly. Partners, parents, children, siblings, in-laws and close friends don't come without their challenges. Confidence can be very rocky when we are trying to sort things out with our nearest and dearest. Family members know just which buttons to press to wind each other up; they created the buttons!

I hope that the many tips and strategies throughout the book will be of help to you in various situations. In this chapter I outline some of life's personal challenges that can result in either reduction or enhancement of your confidence depending on how you deal with them.

Perfect parenting

Congratulations to all of you who have been fortunate in having experienced such luxury as perfect parenting. On the other hand, if your parents abused you either mentally or physically this is really sad and I hope that books like this one can go some way towards helping you to gain and retain the self-esteem that you deserve. At the end of the book you will find references to websites that can direct you to help that is available.

Most of us are able to say that we had good enough parenting, that our parents did the best they could at the time and helped us to become OK adults. In chapter three we focused on the influence of parenting from the child's point of view (see page 22); now I would like to address how to get the balance right in asserting discipline with children confidently and caringly.

Discipline and children

I believe that confidence is at the core of good parenting. Your child loves you. They also trust you. They trust you to take care of them and therefore to know what is best. Yes of course they will, from a very early age, test you out, trying to assert their own way, but please don't forget that you are in charge. They have to wait their turn to be the grown-up and they will only be able to become an effective adult if you have given them some boundaries as a child. Yes, discuss things; listen to their point of view, but in the end you are the one who must have the confidence to make decisions, to say no and to punish if the child has gone over the boundaries. I think a popular term for this is 'tough love'.

Free spirits

You may be familiar with the view of the child as 'tabla rasa', or 'noble savage'; a clean slate of purity upon which life's experiences write an impression. It is a romantic notion and I like to fantasise that in a world of green pastures and sunshine a child can run free, experience nature and humanity and learn and grow within a bubble of protection and innocence. It's not like that though is it?

We have to get to nursery, we have to watch the road, we have to negotiate the supermarket trolley, we have to do swimming lessons and we have to sit tests at school. By the age of seven, children have learned that there are a great number of activities to get through each week. Not much running around fields barefoot is there? This is life as we live it and every child needs a framework of discipline in order to be happy and successful as a child, as an adolescent and as an adult. This is where the responsibility to assert a balanced discipline is at its most crucial. If you choose not to have self-discipline you are the real loser; if you don't assert discipline at work then your career and or business will suffer. But if you fail to create and maintain appropriate discipline with children then you are seriously limiting the potential for your child to have a happy and fulfilling life. Yes, love and nurture their free spirit, give them space to experience and experiment, but do it in a framework of rules and boundaries inside which they feel secure.

It's great to see young children running in a park, playful and carefree. It's irritating to see and hear them running riot in a restaurant or public place. I can cite two recent experiences where people were becoming very agitated with children who were behaving inappropriately: one was in a church, the other in a hospital. Both of them are places with a lot of space and in each case the children were all aged six and under. They were rushing around noisily in just the same way as they would behave in a play area. To some people the behaviour was irritating, to others disturbing and to a few distressing. It was not the children's fault, but it was the children who were blamed. We are not born knowing how to behave in different settings; we have the right to be taught this by our parents. The notion of citizenship is now promoted in schools. Great idea, but I would hope that it is an extension of what people have been taught in the home: that we have a responsibility to behave courteously towards other people with whom we share our world.

Asserting discipline in a healthy, nurturing way involves telling the child what is and what is not acceptable behaviour rather than criticising them in a parent ego state way (see page 22) which can lead them to adopt a negative self-image. When reprimanding a child, try to direct your criticism to their behaviour, not to their whole self. You are showing them that you don't like what they are doing, not that you don't like them.

Have you heard children, when playing together, say 'We're not allowed' in a perfectly neutral way? This suggests that they have been told a certain rule, accepted it and have due regard for that rule. When you hear your children saying this, congratulate yourself. You've done well.

Say what you mean, mean what you say

This is one of the basic principles of assertive communication and essential to setting clear boundaries. If you are going to make a threat to a child then you must carry it through. There is no use saying 'Do that once more and I'll send you to bed' if you don't carry it through. (I personally think bed is a place which should be pleasurable to a child, not an implement of punishment. It's a place that we want them to enjoy being in so that they can charge their batteries and we can charge our own. Somewhere more neutral like the bottom stair can be more effective.) Maybe it is useful to prepare a short list of 'sanctions' to use, which are realistic and relevant. This is helpful because we can find ourselves having to back out of threats if they are unrealistic. For example, 'You won't be allowed to play with Robin' isn't helpful if Robin's mother is just about to drop him off for the morning. Make sure you follow through the threat. Let the child know that the choice is with them: they can either continue the behaviour but pay the penalty, or change their behaviour.

As children grow the boundaries change. Decisions about how much freedom to allow are more complex. There is a need for discussion in which both parties, parents and children/young people, are thinking and communicating in their adult ego state (see page 35). It's perfectly reasonable not to know the answer. A continuous message I have used with my children has been, 'You didn't come with an instruction leaflet. I'm not sure what the best way is here, let's talk it through.' Involving a child in the decision-making will give him/her tools with which to work things out and assert self-discipline throughout life. Of course, there will be times when you have to just come down on one side of a decision and hope it's right. It may not be the popular decision but you have the ultimate responsibility.

Going it alone

Parenting is a joyful experience despite the challenges and occasional heartache. It is hard work though, and I personally think that, ideally, it is a two-person job so long as both people share an attitude and approach which the child sees as consistent. Parenting partners can share the highs and the lows together.

If, for whatever reason, you are parenting alone then be kind to yourself. There is an enormous amount of giving in bringing up a child; make sure that you are also receiving the nourishment required for the job. In workplace situations I often advise people to seek out a mentor – somebody who he or she respects and who they can use as a sounding board. I suggest something similar when you are parenting. Choose somebody who has experience of being a parent but whose children are at different ages and stages from yours. This person can be invaluable in giving you the encouragement and reassurance that is so essential to effective parenting.

Grow their confidence

Everything this book has covered about assertiveness and communication applies to our relationship with children. By giving them an assertive framework they will grow into assertive, confident people who like themselves and are liked by others. They will develop the self-discipline necessary to enable them to negotiate themselves through the education system and to make rational decisions when confronted with the many temptations of young life. They will also have the tools to seek out help and advice and maybe even offer it to others. Listen to them, get to know them, love them a lot, have fun with them and let them know you.

Children are a poor man's gold; treasure them and help them to develop the skills necessary to be a successful human being.

Physical confidence

I confess to having been a bit of a wimp when it comes to adventure. Going back to the theory of Transactional Analysis explained in chapter three (see page 21), I am aware of parental influences on me that were not helpful to my development. I wasn't encouraged to do sport, to push myself physically or to get myself messy and muddy. Consequently, for many years I missed out on a lot of good stuff. I closed myself off to opportunities by dismissing activities such as camping, trekking and other outdoor pursuits. I dismissed such things judgementally but actually it was a lack of confidence that held me back from joining in or trying them out. I guess I was scared of failure, scared of looking stupid and scared of hurting myself.

It is easy to box ourselves in by adopting an attitude about something, but doing so can deprive us of experiences that could prove to be enriching and fulfilling. I know many people whose self-confidence and self-esteem has been hugely enhanced through some kind of physical achievement. Companies use outdoor pursuits for team-building and the results can be life enhancing for individuals who, like me, have been nervous of their physical abilities. It is usually fear itself that troubles us most and once we have overcome that fear it frees us up to try more things.

If you have a physical disability there may be restrictions on what you can actually participate in; the important thing is to be honest with yourself about how much you could actually push yourself to being more active.

Extreme sports are great for those who want to try them but at the other end of the scale just getting out and doing some short walks will help you if that's not what you usually do. It's all a matter of degree; whether you want to increase your fitness to work towards running a marathon or walking a mile. At either end of these scales, enrolling in a charity event which demands getting into a bit of training could be a first step towards building confidence in your physical ability. There are all sorts of spin-offs here of course; as we increase our fitness we feel better about ourselves and so we become more confident and so it goes on . . .

New experiences

New experiences can both challenge and increase your confidence. When did you last do something you've never done before? If the answer to that is 'quite a long time ago', it's time to give yourself a bit of a challenge. Imagine wheeling a bike along a deep rut. It won't get out of the rut on its own; you will need to give it a lift. What can you do to give yourself a bit of lift? What would you like to do that you don't normally do?

Exercise

Rather than dismiss the following list just pause and give each suggestion some consideration. Is it something you might do in order to help your confidence? I'd like you to respond in each case with 'yes', 'maybe' or 'no'.

- Give some time to volunteering.

- Join a local club where they do something you are interested in.

- Enrol in an Adult Education class.

- Go on a trip on your own – a day, a weekend, a week.

- Enrol in an internet dating facility (if you are single, that is!).

- Go canoeing, sailing, surfing or rowing.

- Choose a charity-sponsored walk, run or swim, get a few sponsors and start training for it.

- Make a speech at a party or celebration of some sort.

- Knock on the door of a neighbour you don't know and introduce yourself.

- Invite somebody you like to go for a drink or a coffee with you.

- Go dancing.

- Join a choir or an orchestra.

- Study for a qualification.

- Learn a new skill.

Where you have answered 'no', it's probably because it doesn't appeal, it's not your sort of thing or you don't think it would help your confidence. Fair enough.

Where you have answered 'maybe', I'd like you to think about what would change it to a yes. If it is something that appeals to you then work on removing the barriers that would change a maybe to a yes.

Where you have answered 'yes', think about the practicalities and go for it. Set yourself a SMART goal:

Specific – What will you actually do?

Measurable – How will you know when you've achieved it?

Achievable – Be realistic; if you can't play an instrument then maybe that is the goal rather than joining an orchestra!

Relevant – To you, your lifestyle, your personality and your desire to become more confident.

Timebound – When will you do this and when will you be looking back and congratulating yourself on having done it?

Remember, time is all we've got: make it work for you, not against you.

11 Being a confident consumer

Confidence comes from within us; its roots are in what we are, not what we've got. It is a sad fact that people strive more and more to attain material things and yet, when they get them, they still feel unhappy with themselves. For some people, the bigger their car or house, the fuller their wardrobe or shoe cupboard, the emptier they feel. We can't fill ourselves up with things: they are not what's important during sleepless nights, when we are confronting difficult times or when we are trying to get to grips with real problems.

Over the past two decades our society has become increasingly consumerist. When we go to see our dentist, we are the customer, if we sign on at the job centre we are the customer and hospitals increasingly refer to patients as customers. Managers are told that their staff are their customers. Civil servants and local authority staff are given customer care training in order to meet the requirements of customer charters.

Whatever your view on this development, it brings a change in focus and emphasis which we need to learn to deal with. My view is that generally, British people are not very skilled at being customers; is this because we are subjects not citizens? Neither are we particularly disposed towards giving service – is it something to do with our class system that suggests that servility is demeaning?

When I first visited the USA and Australia I was impressed by the ease with which people delivered good service in shops and restaurants. It made me wonder if, in the UK, there is a fleeting moment in which we assess the status of a stranger before we decide how we will treat them. Do we make an assessment about whether we are in a superior or inferior position to them before we begin communication? Although this idea suggests a cynicism which I am uncomfortable about, nevertheless it does bear out some of my experience of being a customer and also of training people in the skills of customer service.

Watch your language

I am very wary of the term 'retail therapy'. Of course it can be fun buying yourself something new which you look and feel nice in; I'll even grant that it is temporarily therapeutic. But the notion that when your self-esteem is low you might boost it by spending money, is not a sound one. You probably know people who have cupboards stuffed full of items that they will never wear or use, often the spoils of a supposedly harmless session of retail therapy. The alarming thing is that some people will go into debt for this very transient and superficial relief from what? Boredom? Greed? No, I don't think so. Frequently it is from a feeling of discontent stemming from a lack of confidence and self-worth.

A dangerous and unhappy use of shopping to make things better is when people overindulge their children. It is quite common for parents to use material things as a substitute for spending time and really working towards getting to know and understand their children.

So, next time you plan or indulge in 'retail therapy', stop and ask yourself what it's really about. Will it help you – give you the therapy – that you need on this occasion, or is it a way of dodging real issues? Would it be better to spend the time doing something that will lift your spirit, lighten your heart and help you to feel good about yourself? For suggestions on ways to do this see the Quick Reference section on confidence tricks.

Another one of those seamlessly harmless phrases, 'fashion victim', is one that I view with caution. Do we really want to be any kind of victim? I want to be in control of my tastes, my opinions and my creativity in order that I can feel confident in myself and how I choose to present myself rather than feeling the need to keep up with the dictate of an industry. Magazines are fun and attractive to look through. Celebrity gossip can be entertaining and amusing. We must be aware though that this is all presented to us in a format that is all about making profit. Magazines have to be good in order to sell; they have to sell in order that they attract the highest-paying advertisers. If we take these magazines seriously then we can't help but feel discontent with our clothes, furniture, car, sports gear, house, garden . . . It's all in there luring us into getting out to the shops or onto a website to spend money. OK, that's challenging enough, but it's not just things. Body shape and size, skin, hair, teeth, wrinkles . . . The people in the pictures have spent hours being made up, dressed up and lit up in order to look beautiful. They are lovely to look at but not to measure yourself against. You are you and probably, like most people, some bits of you are more physically attractive than others. Make the most of what you've got and enjoy being yourself.

Moaners and groaners

As customers we have rights; as human beings we also have responsibilities. The disease of moaning and whinging but not actually taking positive steps to put things right feeds low esteem and contaminates our life. It obstructs positive attitudes and contributes to many people's 'stamp collection'(see page 49).

I was recently on an intercity train. Halfway into my journey there was a strong smell of burning and within a few minutes we had pulled into a station and been told to leave the train. Almost immediately, people who had avoided eye contact or conversation with one another for hours were united in their rally cry of 'typical', 'this is ridiculous', etc. Almost everybody around me was moaning, yet I felt that it was far preferable to be standing on an airy platform than travelling at high speed in a train that could be potentially dangerous. I stated this to several people, resulting in a graphic example of what happens when we don't make a rapport with others as described in chapter eight (see page 96)!

Moaning about, and belittling, certain services has become a kind of sport for people to indulge in. Maybe having a collective snipe helps people to feel less powerless. I am not suggesting that we should accept bad service or put up with not getting value for our money. I am suggesting that we have the capacity to differentiate between bad service and accidental incidents.

Let's look at the Johnson family. They had saved hard for their holiday in Tenerife and had spent a lot of time poring over brochures to make the right choice of hotel. During the first night of their stay they were disturbed by a variety of noises; this continued on the following nights and it was soon clear that the room they were in was badly designed and would always be subject to noise disturbance.

The family spent their two-week holiday feeling aggrieved and bemoaning their fate to any other guests who would listen. They 'didn't want to upset things' so they did not make a complaint to the hotel or ask to be moved. Consequently they had a miserable holiday, feeling disappointed and angry. They were ratty with one another about the problem and all sorts of other dissatisfactions surfaced about their relationships and their life in general. The hotel may have been aware that the room was below standard but were allowed to get away with it because nobody asked them to do anything. The Johnsons were utterly passive guests/customers.

When they arrived home their neighbour told them that they would be able to claim compensation. Suddenly Mr and Mrs Johnson became very active consumers by writing an indignant letter to the holiday company. Apart from the room problem, they threw in a few other dissatisfactions for good measure in the hope of getting even more compensation.

Of course, they did not receive anything other than a letter of apology from the customer service department. As they had not registered any complaint at the time they were not entitled to anything else. Even if they had been awarded some financial compensation, they couldn't have got their time back, could they? Their failure to deal with the situation assertively at the time resulted in them feeling pretty stupid about it all and less confident about making holiday plans for the future. This is also a prime example of the passive–aggressive swing we find ourselves doing when we don't have the confidence to follow our instinct and sort out things that are not right.

You get what you pay for

At the other end of the spectrum, I recently sat next to somebody on a flight who behaved as though she had bought a first-class ticket even though she was travelling in economy. She made constant demands of the cabin staff, complained about the quality of the food, requested extra pillows and blankets and rang the attendant bell to ask questions about the journey, temperature at our destination and, seemingly, anything else she could think of to make a nuisance of herself. You could say that she was self-confidently asserting herself and ensuring that she got good service, but I say that she was taking advantage of the cabin crew, behaving badly and demanding more than she was actually entitled to.

There is a compromise between these two examples of consumer behaviour. We have the right to get value for money, but we have the responsibility to ensure that we know what we have paid for. If you eat in Joe's Café then you are entitled to receive the service and product promised for the price; the same applies if you eat at the Ritz. Have the confidence to appreciate and enjoy both.

Consumer rights

As a customer, it is important to be aware of consumer rights and to take responsibility to ensure that we get what we pay for. There are numerous books, publications, radio and television programmes to help us with this. I have found the local Trading Standards office and Citizens Advice bureau and their websites useful (see the Quick Reference section on page 163 for website details). Also, many large organisations now publish a 'Customer Charter' or 'Customer Promise' leaflet telling us the standards we should expect and advising how to complain if standards are not met. It is not these formal procedures that this chapter will deal with, but the subtleties of ensuring you get a satisfactory service – something I believe can be achieved through an assertive approach.

The human factor

Television programmes relating horror stories about how people have been treated; whether by builders, restaurants, airlines, hospitals – the list is numerous – have become increasingly popular. I believe they encourage us to complain and assert our rights. Unfortunately though, they don't teach how to do it assertively.

Next time you go into a shop, before making your enquiry, try preceding it with a smile and a greeting: 'Good afternoon. I wonder if you can help me; I'm looking for a . . .' Maybe this sounds rather like the first lesson of a foreign language evening class. I don't mean to be patronising. I firmly believe that this short greeting gets us off to a better start by showing respect to the salesperson, assistant or receptionist. I feel that it is even more necessary when we are going to make a complaint. The ethos is that we are coming together from different angles to meet a need, not that we are opponents prepared for battle. No challenge should be faced without a little charm and a lot of style.

You have the right to ask

Good customer service involves being able to deal well with people and also having efficient procedures. As a customer, there are occasions when we don't know the procedure or the hidden rules of an organisation, and people working there can sometimes make us feel stupid or inferior because we are not aware of how things work. Simple things like queuing systems, self-service machines or terminology can cause us to feel foolish if we allow them to. It is all right not to know, despite the fact that the people serving might treat you as an imbecile. If a receptionist looks over her glasses at you, saying, 'Of course you can't have an appointment straight away', or somebody tells you that a door you have just walked through is private, it is not your fault. The organisation has the responsibility to make procedures and rules clear to their customers.

If, as a family, you go out to eat in a pub or restaurant it is useful to know how long it takes between ordering your food and receiving it. In my experience, staff tend to be defensive about this when you make the enquiry and rarely give you a truthful answer. You have the right to know. If kids are hungry they don't enjoy lingering over a drink while their meal is being cooked. All you need to know is whether you should buy them some crisps or ask for some bread, or whether the meal will be here in five minutes!

I have learned to preface my enquiry with 'I'm not hassling you, just asking, how long is it likely to be before our meal arrives?' Maybe you think it's unnecessary to make yourself amenable to the waiter/waitress, but I see it as avoiding misunderstanding and tempering assertiveness with a little gentleness. Because the general public are becoming increasingly more demanding and often even abusive, people in service jobs tend – sometimes necessarily – to be armed for combat; it is helpful to identify yourself as neutral so that they know you are not the enemy.

The customer is not always right

It is impossible to be truly confident if you are not being truthful. The first honesty must be with yourself. Being confidently in control of your life should help you to discern between things you actually want and things which glossy advertising tells you that you are supposed to want.

Face it, a new 'dream' kitchen is unlikely to make your house bigger, your home happier, or you a better cook. It will fulfil certain needs but when you are buying, it is your responsibility to determine your needs in order to buy well and appropriately. Nit-picking after you have made a purchase because basically you made the wrong decision is not assertive.

- Be sure that you are buying for the right reasons and that you know what you need or want the product to fulfil.

- If you are dissatisfied then the cause of your complaint must be a fault with the product or service, not the decision or choice which you have made.

Stay in control

High-pressure, fast-talking selling is outdated – when confronted with it we quickly hear alarm bells which give us the opportunity to either avoid or slow down the sales pitch. However, there are other tactics and approaches used in sales that make us vulnerable. Once you start to feel yourself wanting to buy something because the sales assistant is 'so nice', 'really helpful' or 'seems genuinely interested in me', beware. If these contribute to your choice to buy then fine, but if they become your reason for buying then you need to take stock of your feelings.

Can you recall a time when, even as you arrived at the till transaction stage, or maybe when you have got the goods home, you have felt a slight unease that you've been seduced by the assistant rather than the product?

You can say no – the situation is not personal, it is a business deal. Whether they are being calculatingly manipulative or they are genuinely interested in you, an astute salesperson can hook your emotions so that you want to please them by buying their products. Here are some useful tactics for staying in control in these situations:

- Calculate how long it takes you to earn that money.

- Think about how often you will actually use/wear/benefit from the item.

- Imagine the sales assistant in your position; think how in control they are likely to be as a customer.

- Remember that if you say no you will be just as important when you walk out of that shop as you were when you walked in.

The rules

If you have purchased goods or services which do not meet their promise then you have the right to complain. If something is faulty, then provided you return it to the place where you bought it within a 'reasonable time of purchase', you have every right to expect a refund. If you have worn, washed, taken apart or further damaged the faulty goods yourself in any way, this may affect your right to a full refund.

If you buy something and then decide that you don't want the goods, the vendor is under no obligation to refund your money or offer you a replacement. Where this does happen it is the policy of the business and is carried out as goodwill rather than legal transaction.

Most stores now give refunds for unwanted goods as a standard customer service policy. If you still have the receipt then you are entitled to a full cash refund. This is the company policy, it is the way they do business, yet it is amusing to stand and watch people's behaviour when they are returning goods. For example:

- 'My aunt bought this for me and it doesn't fit.'

- 'When I got it home it didn't go with the trousers.'

- 'I bought it for a friend and she didn't like it.'

For some reason people appear to feel guilty about what they are doing and have to make an excuse. It is not necessary to do this. It is allowed. It's in the rules; you are not being naughty. If people feel that they must do this in a place where it is made easy to return goods, no wonder they find it difficult in less amenable places. This offers you a good starting place to practise your 'confident customer' skills.

If, in the past, you have been one of those people who always felt they need to give an excuse or explanation then have a go at doing it differently. Walk up to the desk, smile at the assistant, take the goods and receipt from the bag and say, 'I'd like a cash refund please.' Nothing else, just that. Take the money, say thank you and go. That's all there is to it!

Returning faulty goods

At the beginning of this chapter I talked about approach and using a bit of charm. This is never more necessary than when you are going to make a complaint. To begin with, if you go in with all guns blazing then a salesperson is likely to 'take you on'. This might mean sticking rigidly to procedures and going by the book. If your opening gambit is 'I want to speak to the manager' then the salesperson might see the need to watch their back and be defensive or obstructive. Like any situation of conflict, once personal attacks start, it is difficult to separate content from behaviour and things get out of hand. If the salesperson sees you as amenable then they will usually be willing to discuss the problem in order to help find a solution. If you don't get satisfaction from the salesperson then it is appropriate to ask to see a supervisor or decision-maker.

If you begin a complaint in a timid voice, saying 'I'm awfully sorry to trouble you', then it is likely that the person to whom you are complaining will subconsciously start to dismiss the importance of what you are saying. Go back to your plan and remind yourself of your rights. You don't want the other person to think you are a pushover from the beginning. You can remain calm, pleasant and respectful even though you are determined to achieve your outcome. There is no doubt that we are judged by appearance and also that we are influenced by how good we think we look. If you are going to make a complaint give some thought to how you are going to present yourself. Like it or not, people are impressionable and they are more likely to take notice of you if you look well groomed, organised and confident.

Other ways to prepare yourself are:

- Plan what you want to say.

- Rehearse the story if it is complicated.

- Decide what outcome will be acceptable to you.

- Be clear about the details of guarantees or contract agreements.

Once you are in the situation, try the following:

- Take a deep breath and remind yourself that you have the right to get what you pay for.

- Open the conversation with a greeting – announce what you are there for and check that you are speaking to the appropriate person.

- If you prefer not to have an audience, ask if there is somewhere private where you can discuss your business.

- Stay in control of your feelings – this is not a personal issue for either side involved.

Being a customer can be hard work. Sometimes I let things go because I don't feel up to it, see that the front-line person is already under pressure or decide that I don't want to spend time giving somebody feedback on their lack of customer service provision. Once again, if this is your choice then it's fine. But don't be like the Johnsons and spoil precious time by moaning.

The broken record

This is possibly the most widely known assertive technique. Basically it is about deciding on the outcome you want and repeating a statement continuously until you get it! Children are naturally excellent at the broken record: 'Can I go to the park?', 'Please let me go to the park', 'Oh go on, let me go to the park' and so it goes on. Have you been beaten down by this technique? If so, you're in good company. Research on analysis of conversations where this technique is used shows that in the majority of situations the person using the broken record technique gets their way.

Picture the following scenario: Mike bought a pair of shoes a week ago from a small retailer and the stitching has come undone. They have not been subjected to abnormal wear and he has a good case for asking for a refund. He doesn't want a replacement as he is not confident that the same thing won't happen again.

Mike: 'Good morning. I bought these shoes here last week and the stitching has come undone. Here is my receipt and I would like a refund please.'
Assistant: 'We don't give refunds I'm afraid, but I can replace the shoes for you.'
Mike: 'Thank you, but I don't want another pair. I have my receipt and I would like a refund please.'

Assistant: Our policy is to replace shoes if we've got them in stock.

Mike: I understand that that is your policy but I have my receipt and I would like a refund please.

Assistant: The manager isn't here this morning. I can't give you a refund.

Mike: I understand that is a problem for you but I would like a refund please.

Assistant: I could lose my job if I do what you are asking.

Mike: I appreciate your worry about losing your job, but I would like a refund please.

Assistant: If you come back this afternoon the manager will be here.

Mike: I appreciate that you would like me to come back when the manager is here but it is not convenient. I would like a refund please.

Assistant: This is ridiculous, you sound like a broken record.

Mike: I realise that's how I must sound but I would like a refund please.

Assistant: OK, give me the shoes!

Maybe this does strike you as rather ridiculous, but it works! I feel that it needs a bit of gall to do this but on certain occasions, when you have nothing to lose in terms of a relationship it is amazingly effective, as long as you are within your legal rights in your request. I don't advocate it in situations where you need to have an ongoing relationship with somebody as it can feel like aggression if you are on the receiving end. Your voice should maintain the same volume, tone and determination throughout, and you should concentrate objectively on the outcome you want.

Contracting for professional services

So far we have dealt with spontaneous one-off situations. I would like to address the issues involved in longer-term contractual relationships. If somebody is going to supply a product or service to you in a customised way, where you become their 'client', then you deserve to remain as impressed with their performance or product throughout the contractual period as you were when they were trying to sell themselves to you. Take the following examples: arranging a wedding reception, employing people to do building work, choosing a dentist, hairdresser, counsellor or GP, and similar situations where you are going to pay somebody to provide something that isn't readily visible. In business, the examples might include buying in consultancy, training, specialised technology and software. Off-the-shelf goods clearly outline the capacity and features of the product, but it is far more difficult purchasing specialist services. Computer software is a frequent example of this; companies contract software designers to produce certain outcomes for them but can hit problems when the software fails to meet the requirements of the business.

Any contractual relationship should begin by consciously going through the process of the contract and its delivery. For example: you are having an extension built on your home. Some of the things you might check out with the builder before the work starts are the following:

- What date do you expect the work to be finished?

- When do you intend to start?

- Where will your materials be stored?

- What are your working hours?

- What facilities do your workers require throughout the day?

- How many people are likely to be on site?

- Who is responsible for quality and how can they be contacted?

- What are the arrangements for payment – will you require any interim payment for materials etc.?

- What arrangements are there for after-service provision if required?

On commencement of the work, I suggest a discussion on how the workers will conduct themselves and what they can expect from you. For example:

- Precise instructions on what access they have to the house.

- The standard you expect the area to be left in at the end of each day.

- What you will or won't provide in terms of refreshment and toilet facilities.

- What they and you would like to be called.

- Information on pets or children that is helpful for them to know.

- An agreement that if there is a problem, on either side, it will be discussed.

By going through this process everybody knows exactly where they stand and you have set a customer–provider relationship from the start. This might sound cold and humourless, but it doesn't have to be that way at all. If conducted with respect it is usually met with acceptance, willingness to please and a recognition of your confidence. Of course, it is possible, even likely, that they will have something to say about you at their first tea break, but they are probably going to talk about you anyway. At least you will have a less painful few weeks ahead than if people take over your home and you feel too timid to stop them.

Contracting for personal services

A rather different example is when you are selecting somebody for a personal service, such as a counsellor, osteopath or physio-therapist. These are occasions when we can fall into the trap of being intimidated, both by the situation of vulnerability that brings us to the person and by their 'professional' status.

Never forget that you have the right to NOT know something and you have the right to ask questions. Some of the following questions might be appropriate in seeking a helper, whether it is a counsellor for a personal problem or an alternative medicine practitioner for a physical problem:

- What exactly happens in a 'session' with you?

- How often and for how long would you expect me to be coming to you?

- How much will it cost me? When do I pay? What happens if I have to cancel an appointment?

- What experience do you have of dealing with this type of problem?

- Do you have a particular approach?

- Would it be helpful if I read something about . . . ?

- Would you be willing for my partner or a friend to come along with me?

You may find that it is not necessary to ask any of these because the practitioner will go through this kind of information with you as a matter of course. However, giving some thought to what you want to know and preparing the questions will enable you to behave confidently and eliminate any feeling of intimidation you might have.

This is never so essential as when visiting a doctor. Like everything else in life, there are good and bad examples of GPs and consultants. Unfortunately it is often pot luck whether we get somebody good who listens to us and offers clear information and explanation. For many people, going to see their doctor is an experience that makes them feel afraid and inadequate. Add to this their concerns about what might be wrong with them and confidence can go right out of the window!

Always prepare what you want to tell the doctor. Some people suggest writing it furtively on your hand, but I say write notes on a sheet of paper and take it out in front of the doctor. Let them see that you have a list of questions to ask. If you are able to do a bit of research beforehand on your condition and possible treatment available, that can help your confidence. I know doctors are very, very busy people and they may be dealing with patients who are far sicker than you. But you have rights and we have a National Health Service which we pay for. The better the consultation, the less likely you are to waste the doctor's time further by having to go back. Of course we don't have the right to waste a doctor's time. We should be aware of surgery times and not take advantage of the on-call system. But we should use it when essential. Remember, you own your body. It is your responsibility to look after it, but sometimes we need help and we have the right to ask for that help from a doctor. You are their customer: they wouldn't have a job if they didn't have any patients.

In all these situations, remember to stay in control to ensure you get the result that *you* want.

12 Committing to confidence

Throughout this book I have been encouraging you to treat yourself well, to think kindly of yourself and to eliminate destructive, self-critical messages that play in your head. You need to be the best friend you can possibly be to yourself in order that your self-esteem is good and you can be truly confident. I hope, however, that you have also learned that all this doesn't come without effort. Meeting deadlines, achieving goals, getting fit, losing weight, becoming assertive and increasing your confidence all come into the category of 'no pain, no gain'. Just keep remembering: if you do what you always do, you'll get what you always get. If you would like different outcomes, then do yourself the kindness of changing. Assert self-discipline.

The word 'discipline' has different connotations for different people. (I am aware that for some it will evoke an image of Ms Whiplash in all her gear! Fun though it might be to link assertiveness with this, I will maintain discipline and the approval of my publisher by leaving that subject to somebody better qualified.) Generally we associate discipline with order and control, but I fear that it also has a tinge of restraint, punishment and repression about it, which doesn't necessarily fit the 'have it all' society that we have grown to expect. I suppose what I mean is that it's not much fun.

Assert self-discipline but maintain an appropriate balance about it, whether it is with yourself, your kids, your employees or your hobby. Too little discipline and you will not achieve what you want, too much and you create a regime that is harsh and inhibiting rather than creative and relaxed.

Embrace positive stress

An interesting, happy life will involve an appropriate amount of stress to keep us motivated, challenged, interested and interesting. Lack of stimulation and challenge can lead to 'rust out', a form of stress where the lack of demands may lead to boredom, depression and low self-esteem. On the other hand, when work or life in general becomes too challenging and we cannot see a successful resolution of these challenges we suffer a 'burn out' form of stress. At its worst this leads to serious physical or mental illness but even in a mild form it can be extremely debilitating. Once we get out of balance we start to make mistakes, forget things, lose sight of priorities and feel bad about ourselves. See Act on Stress on page 48 for more tips on handling stress.

Take the initiative

Which of these seems right to you?

- It's polite to wait to be asked.

- If you don't ask you don't get.

Being confident involves not waiting to be asked, but taking the initiative and going for it. Never impolitely of course, but certainly with an eye on what you want to achieve and putting the necessary work into action. How often have you said you'd really like to do something but then found an excuse for putting it off? Using the weather, finances, the dark nights, your boss or somebody's attitude – I've no doubt you can add other excuses of your own.

Ask yourself this: Am I the sort of person who does things or the sort of person who talks about doing things? If there is something you want, set your sights, assert some self-discipline and do it.

Exercise

Visualise yourself five years from now. Write down or mentally note the date. Now think about what you would like to be saying on that date about the previous five years of your life. That's it, from now until then. How would you like it to have been?

Well, right now is the beginning of those five years and you have a lot of power to influence how they go. On whatever date it is that you have written down you will have no power at all to influence what has passed. At the moment you have plenty; have the confidence to use it.

Achieve your goals

Work towards achiving your potential and being happy with yourself. Try to:

- know what you want

- set a plan

- assess and develop the necessary skills

- do the work

- monitor your progress

- adjust where necessary

- recognise and celebrate achievement.

This will work best if it really is your goal, compatible with your values and beliefs, and if the outcome is really what you want. We rarely achieve important goals because it is what somebody else wants for us. Whether it is a work or a personal issue, you need to be motivated; you have got to personally want to achieve the goal.

Exercise

Stop reading for a few moments and write down some things that you have got to do.

How does what you have written make you feel?

Now list some things that you want to do.

How does what you've written here make you feel?

It is likely that you feel lighter, more positive, more motivated to do the second list and that you will succeed. Sadly, few of us can go through life only doing what we want so we have to find a way of motivating ourselves.

Doing something difficult

When you need to tackle something that you would prefer not to, do you:

- Put it off by displacement activity? (Such as suddenly tidying your inbox, grooming the cat, checking up on an invoice or transferring information into your new diary, all seeming of greater priority.)

- Exaggerate how bad it will be? (Talking yourself into a scenario where failure is inevitable.)

- Do the easy bits first? (Then become more negative about it because it is now even less appealing.)

- Wish the problem didn't exist? (And consequently focus on the negative to make it even bigger.)

Just writing this has plunged my brain into negative depths making everything seem more difficult! OK, let's have a change of mind.

Take a positive stance

Changing body posture to a positive pose has a powerful effect on the mind. Lift your head up and put your shoulders back. Now take a deep breath and breathe out slowly; as you do so, release any tension you are feeling. Take another deep breath and hold a positive image or word in your mind as you breathe away tension. Continue breathing well, focusing on the in-breath, as it is this one that gives us energy. Hold your head up, maintain that positive thought or image and allow yourself a smile.

Exercise

In this alert but relaxed frame of body and mind I suggest that you return to one of the items you wrote under the 'have got to do' heading. Take an important one and first think about what the benefits will be of finishing this task. Visualise what it will look like or how it will be when it is done. Keep visualising this and focus on how you will feel having achieved it. Now set a plan – where, when, who, how – and ask yourself the following questions:

- What could I do to make this less difficult or tedious? Be creative, maybe there is a different way of doing it.

- What will my internal dialogue be as I am doing the task? Make this positive, encouraging and self-affirming.

- How will I reward myself when it is completed? Make this relevant to the task. A really big one might deserve a weekend away. A smaller task might just earn you a glass of wine in the bath or a pint with a friend. Try to be creative about this; thinking about the reward at the end is a great motivator.

- What will help me to remain positive and focused? Maintain a relaxed body posture. If possible ensure that the ambience around you is pleasant and that you have fresh air and light. I find music really helpful but that will depend upon the setting and the people around you.

Your own success story

By now I hope that you have gained enough confidence to think about writing your own success story. Think about what you've achieved by putting some of what you've learned from this book into practice. What do you intend to do now?

The list below gives examples of general things that people say they are going to do in order to improve their confidence:

- confront problems, not run away from them

- say no when appropriate

- express my feelings

- be realistic about what I can and can't do

- write my own Bill of Rights

- take responsibility for myself

- encourage others to be confident

- be a better friend to myself

- be specific

- evaluate situations

- like myself more

- accept my mistakes.

Exercise

Go back through this list, and for each point ask yourself:

- Will I?

- When?

- What techniques/resources will I use to help myself?

- What will be the benefit to me?

- Will anybody else benefit?

Now add some points of your own.

And finally . . .

However confident you become, the only person you can be in control of is yourself. We don't have control over what somebody else thinks, feels or believes, although we can hope by our words and actions we might influence them. What you *can* control is what *you* think, feel and believe. Yes, this notion is horribly grown-up; it doesn't allow any hiding places where we can deposit blame or responsibility on others. There is, however, a wonderful liberation in this, as it gives us total control over how we choose to behave. Taking responsibility for yourself allows you to be yourself so that you are the driver, not the passenger, in your life's journey.

Personal development is a journey, not a destination. Make sure you are a good travelling companion for yourself – forgive yourself if you get it wrong and celebrate when you get it right. Bon voyage!

Quick Reference Section

Quick reference 1
Confidence tricks

Accept it

There will be times when others see you as a confident person. When they comment on this, hear what they are saying. Accept that the you they see exists and let yourself acknowledge and respect that you.

Anchor it

Think back to a time when you were feeling capable and confident. What did that feel like? Focus on your breathing and bring those feelings to mind when you need them.

Calm it

Do the 'Emergency Stop': breathe, think positively, drop your shoulders and put your brain in gear. *Now* speak!

Enjoy it

Put things into each day, each week and each year that give you pleasure. When you are happy you will be unconsciously confident – the best kind of confidence.

Look it

If you have gone to the trouble of buying new clothes for an occasion, 'make friends' with the clothes so that you enjoy wearing them in a way that looks natural and comfortable.

Monitor it

It might be helpful to you to keep a progress diary. Write down a few situations that you are committed to being more confident about. Maybe start with little things and working up to any 'wet knots'. After you have dealt with one of these, or any spontaneous situation, you can note down:

1. How you handled it – what you did.

2. How you would like to have handled it.

3. What you might do differently next time.

As you gain in confidence and skill you will find that there is little difference between 1 and 2, so that 3 merely acts as a way to refine your skills.

Perform it

As you walk down the street, into a shop or along a corridor, think about what people will see. You will get a positive response from others if your head is up, you smile at passers by and there's a confidence in your stride.

Prepare it

However casual and off-the-cuff they may look, successful people don't just 'blag' it. Whether you have to present yourself to an individual or a group or find your way to a new place, do the preparation. Fail to plan and you plan to fail.

Stand up to it

If you have to make a telephone call which you anticipate will be difficult, confrontational or intimidating, stand up to make the call. Hold your head up as you speak. You will feel and sound more confident.

Quick reference 2
CONFIDENCE

Communicate your thoughts, feelings and needs.

Open yourself up to ideas and new experiences.

Negotiate – be fair but keep sight of your own needs.

Fight for your rights and Face up to your responsibilities.

Influence people rather than trying to control them.

Dare to be yourself.

Expect the best of yourself and of situations.

Nurture the child in you.

Change what you can change; accept what you can't change.

Enjoy being yourself.

Quick reference 3
Further reading and resources

Books

Hobson, B and Scally, M *Build Your Own Rainbow* Cirencester: Management Books, 2000

James, T and Woodsmall, W *Time Line Therapy and the Basis of Personality* California: Meta Publications, 1989

Ready, R and Burton, K *Neuro-linguistic Programming (NLP) for Dummies* New Jersey: Wiley, 2008

Williamson, M and Nicholson, W *The Velveteen Rabbit* London: Harper Collins, 1922; 2008

Zeil, E van der *Perfect Relaxation* London: Random House, 2009

Websites

www.acas.org.uk and www.direct.gov.uk/en/Employment/DiscriminationAtWork for comprehensive information on all aspects of bullying at work.

www.babcp.com for information on Cognitive Behavioural Therapy.

www.bacp.co.uk for details on therapists and counsellors.

www.citizensadvice.org.uk for consumer rights information.

www.do-it.org for information on volunteering opportunities that will help you to build your confidence.

www.europeancoachinginstitute.org for information on finding a life coach.

www.tradingstandards.gov.uk for finding your local Trading Standards office to help with consumer rights.

ALSO AVAILABLE IN RANDOM HOUSE BOOKS

Perfect Detox

Gill Paul

All you need to feel great every time

- Are you concerned that your eating habits are not as healthy as they should be?
- Do you often feel bloated and sluggish?
- Would you like some expert advice on how to detox safely and effectively?

Perfect Detox is is the ideal companion for anyone who wants to give their system a spring clean. Covering everything from 24-hour cleanses to full 30-day programmes, it gives step-by-step guidance on choosing the right detox plan and helpful advice to ensure that you get the full range of nutrients every day. With a unique A–Z listing that includes nutritional information about over 100 detox superfoods, *Perfect Detox* has everything you need to revive and rejuvenate yourself.

The *Perfect* series is a range of practical guides that give clear and straightforward advice on everything from getting your first job to choosing your baby's name. Written by experienced authors offering tried-and-tested tips, each book contains all you need to get it right first time.

BOOKS

ALSO AVAILABLE IN RANDOM HOUSE BOOKS

Perfect Positive Thinking

Lynn Williams

All you need to know

- Are you troubled by negative thoughts?
- Do you find it hard to get motivated?
- Would you like some guidance on how to feel more upbeat?

Perfect Positive Thinking is essential reading for anyone who wants to feel optimistic and enthusiastic. Written by a professional life coach, with years of experience in the field, it gives practical advice on how to overcome negative feelings, explains how to deal with problems like anxiety and self-doubt, and provides helpful tips on how to gain energy, motivation and a sense of purpose. Covering everything from exercising to eating, and from stretching to sleep, *Perfect Positive Thinking* has all you need to feel happy and confident.

BOOKS

ALSO AVAILABLE IN RANDOM HOUSE BOOKS

Perfect Relaxation

Elaine van der Zeil

All you need to keep calm under pressure

- Do you want to take control of your hectic lifestyle?
- Do you want to fight back against stress?
- Would you like some tips on how to be more relaxed?

Perfect Relaxation is an invaluable guide for anyone who wants to learn how to remain calm and powerful in challenging situations. Covering everything from how to stop obsessing to how to start thinking positively, it gives step-by-step guidance on beating stress and shows you how to make relaxation a part of your everyday life. With helpful suggestions for instant calming techniques and daily exercises to help combat tension, *Perfect Relaxation* has everything you need to bring your stress levels under control.

BOOKS